A City by City
Guide to Living
and Working in
Australia

More related titles from How To Books

Getting a Job in Australia
A step-by-step guide to finding work 'down under'

'An indispensable guide for anyone wishing to work in Australia.' – Australian Outlook

Living and Working in Australia
All you need to know for starting a new life 'down under'

'Chock full of advice and pointers for successful entry.' – The Guardian

Getting into Australia
The complete immigration guide to gaining a short- or long-term visa

'Easy to read and to dip in and out of, for that nuts and bolts information, this book is a must-have for all would-be migrants.' – Australian News

howtobooks

Please send for a free copy of the latest catalogue:
How To Books
Spring Hill House, Spring Hill Road,
Begbroke, Oxford OX5 1RX, United Kingdom
info@howtobooks.co.uk
www.howtobooks.co.uk

A City by City
Guide to Living
and Working in

Roberta Duman

Australia

howtobooks

Published by How To Books Ltd,
Spring Hill House, Spring Hill Road,
Begbroke, Oxford OX5 1RX, United Kingdom
Tel: (01865) 375794 Fax: (01865) 379162
info@howtobooks.co.uk
www.howtobooks.co.uk

The right of Roberta Duman to be identified as author of this work has been asserted by her in
accordance with the Copyright, Designs and Patents Act 1988.

First edition 2006
Reprinted 2006

British Library Cataloguing in Publication Data
A catalogue record for this book is available from
the British Library.

ISBN 10: 1 84528 089 X
ISBN 13: 978 1 84528 089 5

Produced for How To Books by Deer Park Productions, Tavistock
Typeset by *specialist* publishing services ltd, Montgomery
Cover design by Baseline Arts Ltd, Oxford
Printed and bound by Cromwell Press, Trowbridge, Wiltshire

Note: The material contained in this book is set out in good
faith for general guidance and no liability can be accepted
for loss or expense incurred as a result of relying in particular
circumstances on statements made in the book. The laws and
regulations are complex and liable to change, and readers should
check the current position with the relevant authorities before
making personal arrangements.

Contents

Preface

More people than ever are contemplating living and working in Australia and who can blame them? Gorgeous weather, stunning landscapes and a booming economy are just a few of its attractions. The wealth of television programmes dedicated to this topic has stimulated many to consider an escape from one (tedious) lifestyle to another (idyllic) lifstyle. However, there is a lack of truly useful and practical information available to those planning to make this move. This became apparent to me when I packed my bags and left the UK to start a new life in Australia three years ago.

This book was written from personal experience in the hope that it will provide you with up-to-date crucial information which will help you navigate your way through the complex aspects of living and working in Australia. It is a truly amazing country and offers a lifestyle that is the envy of countries around the world. The trick is to match your needs with the correct city and ensure that there is a job for you when you get all the way there! I hope that my book makes the relocation process a pleasurable one for you as it certainly will be a memorable one.

I would like to thank my husband Kenan for following me to the other side of the world because I was tired of London! Not to mention his constant support in writing this book and in looking forward to our next adventure. America next?! I would also have been lost without the help of my lovely girlfriend Bunsy who spent many evenings correcting my spelling and grammar, not to mention allowing me to use her incredible photographs. I still owe you a bottle. Thanks also to my best chum Lisa who was the driving force behind 'project fantastic' which lived up to its name.

Roberta Duman

Choosing a foreign exchange company

In recent years there has been a huge increase in the number of foreign exchange specialists who want to help you move your money to Australia. Deciding which one to use can be a daunting prospect, but as Currencies Direct explains there are some simple guidelines that should make the task a little easier, and save you money in the process.

- Select a company that has at least three years of audited accounts and is financially strong.

- Find out more information by doing a quick internet search on the company. Look out for whether they have won any awards or been recommended by a reliable source.

- Do not let a foreign exchange company pressurise you into doing a deal. Their job is to understand your requirements and to provide you with the information you need, not to hard sell and certainly not to make you trade until you are 100% happy.

- Ask what charges apply. If you are unsure, ask them to confirm in writing. You can really save money by using a well established, reputable foreign exchange company; not only through better rates, but also as a result of lower transfer charges. At Currencies Direct all regular transfers are free and one-off transfers are free over £5,000.

- Find out what foreign exchange buying options they can offer you. Some foreign exchange companies let you specify a rate at which you want to buy your currency (limit order) or fix a rate for up to 2 years (forward contract). These can be great tools to help you stick to your budget.

- Be aware that, at present in the UK, commercial foreign exchange is not an FSA regulated industry because it is not considered 'investment business'. Under the Money Laundering Regulations 2003, commercial foreign exchange companies are treated as 'Money Service Businesses' which are covered by regulations administered by HM Customs & Excise.

Information provided by Currencies Direct.
Website: *www.currenciesdirect.com*
Email: *info@currenciesdirect.com*
Tel: 0845 389 1729

PART 1
LIVING IN …

Arafura Sea

Darwin

Gulf of
Carpentaria

Indian Ocean

Wyndham

Derby

Cooktown

Cairns

Coral
Sea

Northern Territory

Townsville

Mount Isa

Mackay

Alice Springs

Queensland

Ayers Rock

Rockhampton

Western Australia

Charleville

South Australia

Brisbane

Geraldton

Bourke

Kalgoorlie

Broken Hill

Perth

Port Augusta

New South Wales

Newcastle

Albany

Adelaide

Sydney

Canberra

Victoria

Melbourne

Indian Ocean

Tasmania

Hobart

1
Why Australia?

WHY LEAVE THE UK?

In today's modern world, travel is increasingly affordable and flights to exotic destinations that were once deemed remote are now reachable at the click of a button. As a nation, the British are travelling further and more frequently than ever before and an increasing number of people are taking the plunge and moving abroad for the simple reason that it is now so much more achievable than it used to be. Technological advances enable people to communicate quickly, cheaply and effectively, ensuring that time differences and distances are no longer the barriers they used to be. The internet and video conferencing now allow people to work from their homes instead of an office, providing opportunities for people to change their lifestyle to suit their own needs and desires. For many, this means they are now in a position to be able to live and work abroad.

In fact, in 2004 alone, nearly 200,000 people left the UK in search of a better lifestyle, warmer weather and the chance of a new, exciting life overseas. By the year 2020, The Centre for Future Studies predicts, a mind-blowing six million more Britons will be living abroad compared with today.

So you are not alone in your thinking! And who can blame you for wanting to leave a country that is over-populated, expensive, becoming increasingly unsafe and has less than desirable weather most months of the year. The world today is a much smaller place than it used to be and making the move to foreign lands is increasingly achievable for you and your family.

Research by Fresh Start has shown that the two of the key factors influencing Brits to move abroad are the climate and the lower cost of living. Australia, definitely can offer both of those, which has ensured that it is, and is set to continue to be, one of the most popular destinations for British migrants.

COST OF LIVING IN AUSTRALIA

For years, Australia was considered a relatively cheap country in which to live but, due to increased tourism, the 2000 Olympics pushing prices up across the board and the continually changing Aussie dollar, Oz is now officially on the high side.

In fact, Australia's cost of living rose faster than anywhere else in the world in the year to March 2004, due mainly to the appreciating Aussie dollar and booming house market (source – Mercer HR 2004. The cost-of-living survey by human resources company Mercer covered 144 cities and measured expenses such as housing, food, clothing, transport and entertainment).

The latest Mercer cost of living study (July 2006) shows that Sydney is still the most expensive Australian city in the country ranking at 19th place, pipping Rome and Los Angeles for cash-draining potential. Melbourne occupies 74th place, while Brisbane is in 99th position with the other Australian main cities not listed on the top 100.

Moscow has taken over from Tokyo as the most expensive city in the world, with London coming not far behind in 5th place.

Mercer's study also revealed that Sydney's housing rents are considerably higher than the rest of Australia and New Zealand.

So, it's official! Sydney is now an expensive city in which to live, especially as wages are much lower than in the UK and taxes are some of the highest in the world. These are key facts which cannot be ignored if you are contemplating making the enormous decision to permanently migrate there.

Having said this, not all of you will be planning on moving to Sydney, and Australia certainly has many more equally exciting and beautiful cities. Increasing number of Brits are shunning NSW's high cost of living and heading to Australia's other large cities including Perth, Brisbane, Adelaide, Hobart and Melbourne, all of which are vibrant and cosmopolitan and considerably less damaging on your pocket. Not to mention the fact that some of the less metropolitan areas of Australia are facing skilled worker shortages, thus creating more opportunities for migrants which in turn may enable you to enter the country via the Regional Skilled Worker Visa (this is discussed in futher detail later in the book and always check www.immi.gov.au for the latest visa information as the situation is ever-changing).

Accommodation

The biggest expense you are likely to incur is accommodation. More than likely you will be renting a property, at least in the first instance. Clearly, rental prices vary enormously depending on location, size etc and there are properties for all tastes and budgets. Sydney and Melbourne are more expensive than other cities, but as a guide you should expect to pay at least a third of your salary for accommodation.

Utilities

In Australia you should expect to pay for the same services as in the UK, ie gas, electricity, phone, internet, etc. Fortunately, it is usually the responsibility of the landlord to pay water and rates.

Schooling

Depending on your visa status, the chances are that most parents will be required to pay schooling fees for children who are non-residents. This can run into thousands of dollars a year per child. Please refer to Chapter 7 for further information.

Entertainment

As with any modern country, the cost of entertainment in Australia varies from cheap to expensive, depending on where you are and what you are doing. You can eat out on any budget and, due to the good weather, many activities take place outdoors and each of the major cities has a wealth of free events for locals to enjoy.

Travel

On the whole, travel is considerably cheaper than in the UK. Public transport (buses, trains, trams and ferries) is a reliable and cost efficient way of navigating your way around the cities and suburbs. Taxis are very reasonable and it is unlikely that any local journey will break the bank, unlike the black cabs of the UK. If you are considering purchasing a car, then do shop around, as new vehicles in particular are not cheap, especially imports.

Personal items

Clothing and toiletries are average prices, and all tastes and budgets are catered for.

Groceries

Many of the items found in the shops are locally produced and therefore priced competitively. The quality of meat and fish is second to none and the range is incredible. Some fruits and vegetables that are imported from overseas are particularly expensive but, on the whole, groceries are affordable.

Price comparisons

Things you'll find cheaper than in the UK:

- Fresh meat and fish – seafood is cheap and of fantastic quality, as is the meat.

- Transport is very reasonable and of a high standard, particularly in the larger cities.

Things you will find more expensive than in the UK:

- Despite the fact that it is locally produced, wine is not cheap in Australia, either to purchase in stores or in bars/restaurants.

- Schooling – especially if you do not currently pay for your children's education.

- High quality menswear appears to be harder to find than women's and on the pricey side.

GST

GST is a tax on goods and services that at the time of writing stands at 10%. It currently excludes food.

AVERAGE WAGE

In 2004, according to the Australian Bureau of Statics (ABS):

- The average annual Australian wage stood at $49,000 AUD.

- After tax, a worker on average wages takes home $37,423 a year, or $720 a week.

At today's exchange rate this is the equivalent of £15,600 GBP.

Before you panic and worry that you cannot afford to work in Australia, you should be aware that for skilled workers and management, your potential earning power can well exceed the national average and allow you and your family to live more than comfortably.

UNEMPLOYMENT

In February 2006, the unemployment rate was 5.2% which is marginally higher than in February 2005 (5.1%) (source: Australian Labour Market Update April 2006). The unemployment rate was highest in the Northern Territory at 7.1% and lowest in the Australian Capital Territory at 3.3%.

The unemployment rate for migrants varies according to their country of origin. The current UK and Ireland rate is below the Australian average at under 4%, which is promising for those considering migration to Australia to work.

SO WHY LIVE AND WORK IN AUSTRALIA?

Despite the lower wages, there is no doubt that Australia is a highly desirable place to live. In a separate survey of 215 cities, research carried out by leading company Mercer found that Australian cities continued to rate among the highest for quality of life with criteria including; political, social, economic and environmental factors, personal safety and health, education, transport and public services. Sydney, Melbourne, Perth, Adelaide and Brisbane all feature within the top 25, ahead of cities like San Francisco, Paris, London and Montreal for all-round health, safety and good times. In 2004 Melbourne moved up from 15th place to 12th due to improved law enforcement.

Although the Australian visa process is complicated and time consuming, skilled British workers are considered a strength to the country's economy. Providing that you meet certain criteria, there is no reason why you cannot earn a good living in Australia and I challenge anyone not to enjoy the stunning scenery and incredible weather. It's not without good reason that the country is also one of the most popular destinations in the world for international visitors. The Australian lifestyle and stunning climate ensure that it attracts endless numbers of Brits, some of whom never leave after visiting and falling in love with all it has to offer. Despite being the sixth largest country in the world, Australia has a lot of space but not many people. It has the lowest population density in the world – only 2.5 people per square kilometre – a far cry from the packed cities of England! Aussie lifestyle is arguably the finest in the world and is the number one reason that most people flock to its sandy shores to live and work.

If life in Australia is appealing to you, continue reading, do lots of research and start saving those precious pounds for the ultimate trip down under!

2
Australia – An Introduction

Full name: Commonwealth of Australia
Area: 7.68 million sq km
Population: 20,682,467 (est March 2006)
Capital city: Canberra
Language: English
Government: Independent Member of the Commonwealth
of Nations
Head of Government: Prime Minister John Howard

THE PLACE

Australia is the sixth largest country in the world. In addition to the
mainland, it is surrounded by many thousands of small islands and
numerous larger ones. Australia is nearly 50% larger than Europe, but it
has the lowest population density in the world – only 2.5 people (and
many sheep and kangaroos) per square kilometre. This is due to the fact
that despite the abundance of land in Australia, there are very few
inhabitable areas in the middle of the country. Most people live on or near
the coast, leaving the centre virtually empty.

Surrounded by the Indian and Pacific Oceans, Australia is a country of
stunning natural beauty – the evidence of which is visible at every turn.
Whether you live by the beach or in the city you will be spoilt for things
to do and sights to see. The sunsets are breathtaking, the landscapes are
dramatic and the architecture is astounding. Australia truly is a diverse

country. There are not many places in the world that have endless golden beaches, dazzling mountains, tropical rainforests and exotic coral reefs all within a stone's throw of the nearest cosmopolitan city or local town.

Australia is often referred to as the 'Lucky Country'. And compared with many others round the world it certainly is lucky. It is a peaceful country that is proud of the rare fact that it has never had a civil war or had to fight for territory. The government is democratically elected, not ruled by the military and does not face any major political or religious issues. These facts, combined with the country's spaciousness, excellent standards of living and pleasing climate, ensure that Australians experience a peaceful and high quality of life that is envied around the world.

The country consists of six states and two territories: New South Wales, Queensland, South Australia, Tasmania, Victoria, Western Australia, Northern Territory and Australian Capital Territory.

This book will discuss living and working in all of the six states and Tasmania. However, the Northern Territory (NT) has been omitted for several reasons. Not only does it have the smallest population in Australia (approximately 165,000 which accounts for less than 1% of the country's population) meaning that there are few opportunities for skilled workers, but the state capital of Darwin's economy has suffered in recent years. In addition, NT does not offer the same pleasant living conditions as so many other parts of the countries as the climate is tropical with incredibly hot temperatures all year round. Sydney is Australia's largest city, followed by Melbourne then Brisbane.

THE HISTORY

Aboriginal Australia

The 'Aborigine' people have the longest continuous cultural history in the world, with origins dating back to the Ice Age. There is some disagreement between historians as to precisely when the first Aborigines arrived in Australia by sea from South East Asia, but it is estimated to be around 50,000 years ago. The Aborigines became part of the land they lived in and survived in hostile conditions in areas of Australia that might be considered uninhabitable. They were nomadic hunters and lived off what nature provided for them.

When the first Europeans came to Australia there were around 750,000 Aborigine people (or 'primitive natives' as the white folk rudely called them) who were happily living at one with the land that had been their home for thousands of generations. The Aborigine people consisted of around 500 tribes, each with their own dialect or language.

The Europeans

Portuguese and Spanish explorers often chanced upon Australia's shores by accident, reporting back to their governments about a vast new land. This paved the way for new and ambitious explorers to take to the seas and in the late fifteenth century the Dutch set their sights on the southern hemisphere in search of new riches. It was Dutch captain William Jansz who discovered the Cape of York in 1606 but, claiming the land was too dry and arid to be of any commercial worth, sailed on. Some 60 years on British seaman William Dampier landed on the northwest coast in 1688. He was soon followed by the infamous Captain James Cook, who extended a scientific voyage to the South Pacific in order to chart the east coast of the continent that had become known as 'New Holland'. On 23 August 1770, after landing at Botany Bay (Sydney), Cook claimed the land for the British Crown and named it New South Wales. The plans were to establish this area as a new penal colony for petty British convicts.

When Captain Cook and the British arrived, the area around Sydney

Harbour was occupied by around 3,000 Aborigines. Cook documented that his men were met with 'warriors with spears' who threatened them.

There was little attempt to understand the Aborigine people or their culture and beliefs. They were seen as primitive people who stood in the way of British colonisation. Sharing the land with the Aborigines was never an option for the British and, when they returned, they set upon a deliberate and destructive campaign to clear them from the country which continued for many years. Many died from the introduction of new diseases, such as smallpox, to their country and others were murdered or poisoned. Within just a few decades, the British managed to wipe out nearly an entire race of people who had peacefully lived in Australia for thousands of years.

The British started sending convicts to Australia in 1788, to the newly named area of Sydney. Over the next 30 years many more European settlers arrived and were encouraged to move further afield and establish new communities. New South Wales was opened up to free settlers in 1819 and by 1858 they ceased importing convicts to the country, which by this point was becoming a popular destination for immigrants. In the years since, Sydney Harbour has continued to play an important part in the development of the nation.

The development of a nation

On New Year's Day in 1901 The Commonwealth of Australia was created when the six colonies, namely New South Wales, Victoria, West Australia, Tasmania, South Australia and Queensland, were federated to form one nation. During the development of the federal state Sydney and Melbourne argued over which of them should become the country's capital. As a result of this Australian Capital Territory was created in New South Wales and the new capital Canberra was born. However, it took many years to plan and build the new city, therefore Melbourne was declared the nation's capital until the building of Canberra was completed in 1927.

In the decades since, Australia has continued to embrace settlers from other countries and is now one of the most multicultural countries in the world.

Although Australia is an independent nation, Queen Elizabeth II of Great Britain is also formally Queen of Australia. In recent years there has been much discussion about replacing the Queen with Australia's president and making Australia a republic. This was considered such an important issue to the Australian people that in November 1999 11.6 million voted in a referendum that could have ended Australia's formal allegiance to the British Crown. However, the majority of the nation voted 'no', so there were no changes to the Constitution. Clearly this is a subject that will continue to be discussed in both the public and private spheres of Australian society, especially as the constitutional ties to Britain are lost by the younger generations.

ATTRACTIONS

It is not without reason that Australia has become one of the most popular tourist destinations in the world. Its attractions are too vast to detail and the landscapes are too breathtaking to adequately describe on paper. Aside from the many iconic landmarks that Australia is globally famous for, including Ayers Rock (also known as Uluru) and the Sydney Opera House, the country's biggest asset comes from its diverse and natural beauty. Wherever you may be, you are never far from a point of outstanding beauty whether it be a lake, beach or rainforest. Each sunset offers a constant reminder of the amazing riches that Australia has to offer. The vibrant cities have the cosmopolitan chic of many European counterparts but without the hectic pace and aggression of other major cities.

The climate

In Australia the seasons are reversed from those in the northern hemisphere. In general temperatures vary enormously throughout the country and in the summer months it can get incredibly hot in some areas; however, most cities are balanced by the seasons. Even in the depths of winter it rarely hits freezing point anywhere in the country, though Tasmania and of course the mountains may be exceptions.

- spring starts in September
- summer starts in December
- autumn starts in March
- winter starts in June.

There aren't many countries where you can ski, dive with whale sharks, walk in the tropical rainforests and sunbathe on the beaches on any day of the year.

Quality of living

The country is economically and politically stable which makes it a particularly attractive place to live in today's uncertain times. In addition, Australia is currently enjoying high growth, and low inflation and interest rates. When combined with a buoyant labour market that values skilled overseas workers, this makes Australia a hugely desirable destination for British people seeking a slice of the good life. It truly is a land of opportunity and welcomes migrants to its shores, so get packing!

Security

Not surprisingly, Australia has a lower crime rate than England and violent crime is not common.

In fact in recent years, statistically crime is on the decline in Australia. As with any country in the world, you should still take precautions to secure and protect your property and yourself. If you are careful it is unlikely that you will be affected by crime.

USEFUL GENERAL INFORMATION

Time zones

Due to the fact that Australia is such a vast country it has three time zones. This can be a little confusing, especially when only certain states across the continent change to Daylight Saving Time (late October to late March), marking the official beginning of summer. In order not to confuse you unnecessarily, on arrival at your chosen Australian city ensure you immediately become aware of the time zone in your area and work out how many hours you are ahead of the UK. If in doubt, refer to www.abc.net.au/backyard/timezone.htm

Business hours

Main shopping hours are weekdays, 9.30am to 6pm; Saturdays, 10am to 5pm. Thursdays are late night shopping hours with most of the larger shops opening until 9pm. The banks are still somewhat traditional in their hours in Australia – most opening from 9.30am to 4pm, Monday to Thursday, and 9.30am to 5pm on Friday. Some are now open on Saturday mornings which paves the way for others to follow. Unfortunately post offices are not yet open at the weekends. Supermarkets in residential areas close between 8pm and midnight. It seems that 24-hour shopping has yet to reach most of Australia!

Emergency services

For police, ambulance and fire services: dial 000.

Currency

The currency is the Australian dollar, made up of 100 cents. Coins come in five, ten, 20 and 50 cent pieces and 1 and 2 dollar units. Notes come in 5s (purple), 10s (blue), 20s (red), 50s (yellow) and 100s (green).

3
The Australian Way of Life

THE PEOPLE

Australia is ethnically diverse and home to people from over 140 countries. As a nation, Australians are very accepting of people from other cultures and thankfully for us they welcome migrants to their shores. Of course it does help that they are blessed with such a huge land so sharing with others doesn't lead to conflict as it can do in other countries.

Australians are proud of their country and enjoy showing allegiance to it, especially during international sporting events! Despite the vastness of the country, they enjoy coming together to celebrate national events such as Australia Day and unite in times of need. However, they are not aggressively patriotic, unlike some other nations. They are proud of their soldiers, in particular the old servicemen, and turn out in thousands on Anzac Day to remember those who lost their lives.

They are also a cheerful and social bunch who are on the whole very laid back. They tend to look on the bright side of life and think that most things can be fixed easily, especially if it's done over a beer. Should you need a hand with directions, or anything else for that matter, most Aussies are happy to stop and help. Chivalry is not dead as, I'm pleased to say, they happily give up their seats on public transport for those in need. They are opinionated and their directness can sometimes be interpreted as rudeness; however, this is unintentional (most of the time).

They are eco friendly and take pride in their beautiful country and understandably do their best to preserve it. Their parks and beaches are spotless, as are their streets, and people tend to tidy up after themselves as littering is considered taboo.

Brit tip

The Australians tend to dress down – this has a lot to do with the weather and their laid back attitude to life. Do observe their culture and work out what is appropriate for work and leisure.

GAY AND LESBIAN AUSTRALIA

On the whole the country is gay and lesbian proud and sexuality is not an issue to most Australians, particularly in the cosmopolitan cities of Sydney, Melbourne and Brisbane. Every March Sydney is home to the notorious and stunningly flamboyant Mardi Gras Festival – the highlight of which is the parade through the suburbs in which over a million people turn out to watch the floats and spectacular sights on offer. It truly is a once in a lifetime experience that is shared by people from all walks of life including families. Other festivals take place at various times throughout the year across Australia.

www.galta.com.au

THE AUSSIE LANGUAGE

Although the 'native' language in Australia is English, you may question this fact after spending some quality time with an Aussie, especially when trading stories with them over a 'tinny' or two (a beer to you and me). Whilst most of the words they use are familiar, there are more than a few Australianisms that need a word or two of explanation. The Aussie accent also has a twang that tends to go up at the end of a sentence, leading you to think that everything is a question. If you have a strong British regional accent they, too, might think you sound strange so fair's fair. See my slang guide (page 269) to ensure that you know precisely what is being said to you and for some ideas on what to say back!

THE LIFESTYLE

It should come as no surprise that Australians love being outside. Who can blame them for making the most of the incredible weather or beautiful surroundings? With the abundance of beaches, nature parks, reserves and forests there are endless outdoor activities to be enjoyed and the Aussies truly do make the most of them.

The country has stunning beaches and wherever you live in Australia it seems that you are never far from the surf. Most locals have grown up with one foot in it and, to many, being in or on the sea is a crucial part of daily life. Surfing is considered a religion for the devoted thousands who are up at the break of dawn, day in day out chasing waves around the country. It is not confined to the young, as people of all ages and from all walks of life can be found popping up and down like seals, come rain or shine.

Brit tip

Australia has one of the highest incidences of skin cancer in the world. The ozone is particularly thin over the country therefore burn times are extremely short. Most British people will be unaccustomed to the strength of the sun. Ensure that sun protection becomes part of your daily routine and follow the government's recommendation of 'Slip, Slop, Slap' which encourages people to use high factor sun screen, and to wear a hat and cover up when spending long periods in the sun.

There are also endless parks, reserves and lakes in and around the cities, all of which offer numerous leisure opportunities including running, cycling, riding, swimming and walking.

THE ANIMALS

Australia has an incredible and diverse range of wildlife that of course includes the famous koalas, kangaroos, wombats, kookaburas and dingos that so many people associate with the country.

Australia has many of the deadliest animals in the world including snakes, sharks and spiders. Few people know that even the cute looking platypus produces one of the most excruciating venoms known. This aside, there is no reason why you should ever be aware of this fact, as you shouldn't come across the deadly varieties on a daily basis. Unless you visit the zoo or aquarium you are unlikely ever to see them as, in most cases, they don't wish to be found.

In the air

You will become accustomed to daily sightings of what we in England would consider exotic birds including parrots, cockatoos, parakeets and pelicans. If you can't see them you will almost certainly hear them! They are in abundance, even in cities, all across the country, not to mention the fruit bats that live in the trees of national parks and gardens. You will also learn the familiar laugh of the Australian icon, the kookaburra, which is a large 'noisy' bird found throughout the country.

In the water

There are over 300 species of sharks in Australian waters. Most are not dangerous to humans; however, the fearsome great whites are present in some waters, but rest assured that shark nets are in use in many of the country's popular swimming beaches.

During the migration season whales can be spotted in key coastal areas throughout the country, as can turtles and seals. In other waters, in particular northern rivers, crocodiles are present so caution must be used when travelling in unfamiliar territories. At various times of the year it is not safe to swim in the ocean (particularly in tropical North Queensland) without wearing a 'stinger suit' due to the potentially fatal box jellyfish that are present in the waters. However, you are far more likely to see a beautiful variety of marine life including sting rays, dolphins and exotic fish than anything sinister.

Brit tip

Far more dangerous than what may be lurking in the water is the ocean itself. Rip tides are common and you must observe the warnings present on all swimming beaches. Do not swim outside of designated areas.

On the ground (or more usually in the trees)

Adored around the world, the koala is an Aussie icon. Sometimes mistakenly called koala bears, they are in fact marsupials. Their staple diet is eucalyptus leaves and they are protected by the state and considered a national treasure. Aside from the national parks, they can be found in the cities but you will need a trained eye to spot them as they are usually asleep at the top of tall trees. Kangaroos can be spotted in more rural areas where you are also likely to see wombats and possums.

AUSTRALIANS AND SPORT

It is not without good reason that people around the world associate Australia with sport.

The fact is Australians are a sports obsessed nation and your typical Aussie isn't shy of letting you and anyone else within earshot know it! As a country they are also globally recognised for producing some of the world's most successful competitors across many different sports including swimming, cricket, rugby, rowing, volleyball and tennis. Their sports men and women are national heroes and are worshipped by the public and the media. Aussies regularly turn out in enormous numbers to (loudly) support the competitors and games. It is not surprising that such a sporting country also boasts some of the most impressive facilities and stadiums in the world, many of which are the result of the phenomenally successful 2000 Olympics.

The Aussies also enjoy nothing better than taunting us Brits about our nation's sporting achievement (or lack thereof!).

Rugby

Rugby is one of the most popular sports in Australia, existing in three forms: Rugby Union, Australian Rules and Rugby League. Actually, despite the fact that they look alike, each one has many different rules. Rugby has the same importance for an Australian that football has for the Brits.

The footy

One thing you cannot escape when living in Australia, particularly in Melbourne, is their one truly original home grown sport. Known affectionately as the 'footy', AFL stands for Australian Football League and is a hugely entertaining sport. Each team has 18 players and contrary to popular belief, this game does have rules, although it might take some time to work out what they actually are. All I could gather is that it seems to involve kicking an oval ball as far down the pitch as possible… It is played in four quarters lasting 20 minutes each, and the constant punch-ups on the pitch add to the game's excitement and ensure the crowds come back week after week in their thousands. The game is Australia's premier spectator sport with an average of 14 million people turning out to games annually. Not bad figures considering that only 20 million people live in the country! Known locally as Aussie Rules, the game is unique in the fact that it requires hand and foot skills, strength, co-ordination and athleticism in equal proportions.

Cricket

The cricket season brings with it a wealth of opportunities for Aussies to spend a fun day sitting in the stands with their friends and it is responsible for more than a few 'sickies' being thrown. Thousands turn out for the one-day games and longer test series and the locals are easily recognisable as they usually have a pie in one hand, a cold beer in the other and zinc cream all over their faces. It's a rather lively affair, as most sporting days out in Australia are, and it's usual practice to give the umpire a hard time, but it's all done in good spirits and there's rarely, if ever, any trouble despite the beer being in constant flow. Aside from watching the cricket, the Australians love to play the game themselves and it is not uncommon to see families and friends playing at parks and beaches at the weekends.

Tennis

Every January thousands flock to Melbourne for the Australian Open to see the biggest names on the international circuit go head to head for this grand slam tournament. Just as we get behind our British hopefuls at Wimbledon, the Aussies take this opportunity to be swept up in patriotism and back their players in their unique and vibrant style, ensuring that it's always a fun and exciting sporting event on their bumper packed annual calendar.

Football

Football is generally known in Australia as 'soccer'. It does not have a particularly high profile in the country, primarily because their national team (called the 'Socceroos'!) does not have an international reputation for excellence. However, the game is gaining popularity and is played widely across the country, particularly in the amateur leagues at weekends. British football fans need not worry about keeping abreast of their local teams as both English and international games are featured on Australian television!

www.footballaustralia.com.au

FOOD AND DRINK

Modern Australian food

Australian food used to have a terrible reputation as being like British food but noticeably worse! This is certainly not the case today. In fact, the standard of food is extremely high and there are culinary delights to be tasted throughout the country, particularly in Melbourne and Sydney. As Australia is a multi-cultural nation, the food reflects the wide range of influences and tastes that are present, ensuring there is something to tantalise everyone's taste buds.

Australians (like most people) place a great emphasis on food throughout their lives. As a nation they have few native foods; however, it is not uncommon to find the likes of kangaroo on the menu. Meat is extremely popular, largely due to its low cost and availability as Australia is one of the world's largest meat producers. The quality and diversity of sea foods will have you in awe as will the size of the shellfish! The majority of Australia's food is locally produced and you really do notice this in the taste.

As with most other countries, food is a way of life and is an experience to be shared with friends and family. The rumours about Aussies loving a good barbeque are true, and who can blame them for wanting to be outdoors as much as possible when the weather is so reliable and the scenery is as stunning as it is across the country. Most parks and beaches have barbequeing facilities which are put to good use, especially in the summer months. Many restaurants offer *al fresco* dining and it's amazing how good a cold beer and bowl of chips can taste whilst looking across the beach, or harbour, at a wonderful sunset.

Traditional Aussie tucker

You won't be able to live in Oz and escape some of the traditional favourites which are still on many menus, including the 'meat pie' which is popular in restaurants and fast food joints across the country and comes with the option of peas and gravy (known as a 'floater'). 'Vegemite', their equivalent of Marmite, is another Aussie tradition that you will come across and which they spread on anything.

Drink

Due to the warm climate, drink is also considered very important by the Aussies. Wine is produced in huge quantities due to the favourable growing conditions, and various regions including Margaret River, The Hunter Valley and Adelaide Hills are responsible for making some of the world's finest reds and whites. Beer is also considered an important part of Aussie culture, especially with males, and goes hand in hand with sporting events. Australia has many beers including national ones such as Tooheys and Carlton, and then there are the state varieties – one of the most popular being Victoria Bitter (VB). Next door to most Aussie pubs are 'Bottleshops'. These are basically off licences and the main place to purchase alcohol, known locally as 'grog', as it is not sold in supermarkets. There are also plenty of drive throughs, particularly in regional areas, which are very handy for picking up your tinnies!

Restaurants

Australia has a huge variety of restaurants catering for all tastes and budgets. Many take advantage of the weather and have outdoor dining facilities. It is also common in Australia to offer a BYO (bring your own) policy. This means that patrons are welcome to bring their own alcoholic beverages including beer and wine. This means that your bill is considerably less and you can afford to spend more on high quality foods instead of paying huge marks-ups on wine lists. Some restaurants charge 'corkage' of about $1 or $2 per person if you bring your own alcohol but in most cases it's more than worth it.

Brit tip

- Tipping is *not* added on to bills in most establishments apart from those at the higher end and is generally left to your discretion. In smaller, family run restaurants and BYO this usually means that any money you leave goes directly to the staff who served you instead of lining the pockets of the owners as is often the case in the UK.

- Australian beer measurements are different from ours and vary depending on which state you are in. Beer and lager on tap in pubs and bars comes in a variety of sizes and it can be confusing to us non-locals – check with the bar staff when ordering otherwise you might get something you didn't want.

- Despite Australia being a large producer of wine, it is on the pricey side, especially for premium brands. To save money take advantage of great deals online or go to larger discount stores such as Liquorland.

4
Getting Around Australia

IN THE AIR

International

All major airlines offer routes in and out of Australia and as tourism to the southern hemisphere continues to boom, fares have become increasingly affordable. Prices will vary across the airlines and are affected by the seasons, with the Christmas period generally being the most expensive. Each of the State capitals has at least one airport, as do many smaller towns. Indeed in some remote areas of the country air travel is the only way to reach some towns and there is a Flying Doctor service.

> **Brit tip**
>
> When in Australia, Flightcentre offers competitive prices on all domestic and international flights. They will offer to match any fare found, ensuring that you achieve the best deal possible. They have branches across the country, or refer to www.flightcentre.com.au or call 133 133.

Domestic

Thanks to the introduction of Richard Branson's Virgin Blue and the more recent arrival of JetStar (launched by Qantas to compete against

Branson), domestic air prices are at all-time lows as the airlines battle for dominance of the skies. Both of these airlines operate multiple routes across the country and the Tasman sea and are continually expanding their routes as demand for low fares increases. As you would expect from these corporate giants, both offer efficient services at excellent prices, enabling both locals and visitors to make the most of the sights and cities that Australia has to offer.

Brit tip

Check both of these websites regularly for special offers and sign up for their online newsletters as they regularly run promotions which can save you valuable dollars:

• www.jetstar.com.au

• www.virginblue.com.au

ON THE GROUND

Trains

Australia's trains are clean and comfortable and, on the whole, the service is efficient and fairly priced. All major cities across the country have rail links, some operating to smaller rural towns, and there are some breathtaking scenic routes to be experienced.

Brit tip

On most trains one section will have a guard present at all times or late at night, ensuring the safety of passengers. Women in particular should look out for the signs indicating where these compartments are.

Buses

The bus network in Australia is extensive and covers most destinations in the country. Buses are clean and comfortable with essential air conditioning. Do bear in the mind the size of the land when travelling as some journeys can take days, so ensure that you are prepared for the trip.

Useful national coach operators:

Greyhound Pioneer Australia. www.greyhound.com.au (no relation to Greyhound in the USA).

www.busaustralia.com

Driving

If you own a vehicle you really can experience the riches of Australia, as you can reach the places off the beaten track and away from public transport routes.

Compared with the UK, driving in Australian cities is, on the whole, a pleasurable experience. The roads are well maintained and they simply do not suffer from the congestion and traffic that are the cause of so much frustration in other countries. However, in some rural areas some places can be hard to access without a four-wheel drive as dirt roads are common.

Brit tip

- When planning a journey that is on unfamiliar roads or terrain, purchase an up to date map and ensure that you have a vehicle that is suitable for your trip, as you could easily find yourself on a route that can only be accessed by four-wheel drives.

- Do make sure that you have water and a spare tyre, and never leave your vehicle especially if you are not familiar with the area. Make sure someone knows that you are travelling so that they can raise the alarm if necessary.

Speed limits are 50-60 kilometres per hour (kph) in populated areas, and 100-110 kph on open roads – the equivalent of 31-37 and 62-68 mph, respectively. There are no speed limits on the open road in the Northern Territory. Limits in school areas are usually around 40 kph (25 mph). Surveillance of speeders and drink-driving (the legal limit is a tough .05% blood-alcohol level) is thorough, and penalties are high. Seat belts are mandatory nationwide for drivers and all passengers.

Renting a car

- Avis. www.avis.com.au
- Budget. www.budget.com.au
- Hertz. www.hertz.com.au
- Thrifty. www.thrifty.com.au

OBTAINING AN AUSSIE DRIVING LICENCE

You only really need to obtain an Australian driving licence if you take up Permanent Residency as your British one is acceptable for car rental.

If you enter the country with a permanent visa you are allowed to drive on your UK licence for the first three months after becoming an Australian resident. After this you will be required to change to an Australian driver's licence. As in the UK, you will need to pass a knowledge test, an eye examination and in some cases a driving test. However, Australia recognises countries that have comparable licensing standards to Australia (including the UK) and if you are applying for a class C (car) licence and hold a current UK licence, or one that expired within the last five years, you should not be required to take a driving test.

For information on the Australian driving test refer to: www.licencequest.com.au

---

Brit tip

- The Australian police are serious about driving offences. Do carry your licence with you when you are driving as they will fine you on the spot if you do not have it.

- Do be observant of speed limits – they vary across the country and speeding offences carry hefty penalties.

OWNING A CAR

You can purchase a car easily in Australia and you will be familiar with most of the makes and models on offer. Prices are competitive and do shop around for deals.

To drive a car legally on Australian roads you must register the car. This procedure can vary throughout the States. In general, in order to do this you must have:

- Proof of your identity.

- Proof of how the car is in your possession or proof of how you bought the car.

- A current compulsory third party or green slip – this is the most basic form of car insurance and all you need to drive legally. However, this only covers third party medical costs. It does not cover damage to your own vehicle, nor to the third party's. Additional insurance is not required, though, obviously, it might be wise to take some out.

- A pink slip – the equivalent of a UK MOT certificate – which is an inspection report verifying that your car is in good enough condition to be used on the roads.

- You will also need to pay an annual registration ('rego') fee which is the equivalent of our car tax and is a legal requirement.

5
Finance

TAX

Australia has an incredibly high taxation system – a fact few people realise before they arrive in Australia.

Tax File Number (TFN)

A TFN is a unique number issued by the Australian Tax Office (ATO) to individuals for identification and record-keeping purposes. Anyone who intends to earn money in Australia, regardless of age and nationality, needs to apply for a TFN. If you do not have a TFN you may have more tax withheld than is necessary when you start earning, so it is advisable to get one as soon as you can after you have settled.

How to apply for a TFN

TFN application forms are available from the ATO or Centrelink offices. You can also phone the tax office between 8am and 6pm, Monday to Friday on 13 28 61 to make an appointment.

What documents do I need?

If attending the office in person, you will need to provide original documents proving your identity. The TFN application lists the types of documents accepted by the ATO. You should receive your TFN within four weeks of your application.

You can also now apply online for your TFN, which may be more convenient as no identification documents will be required. You can apply via their website at www.ato.gov.au

Select 'For individuals' then go to 'Online individual tax file number (TFN) registration'.

When you start working

Your new employer will ask you for your TFN so that their payroll can determine how much tax to take out of your payment. It is to your advantage to have one already in place as providing this information should prevent you from being charged the maximum rate (currently 48.5% plus a Medicare levy). However, you will have 28 days from the day you start work to give your TFN to your employer before tax is deducted at the maximum rate.

Residency (for tax purposes)

Generally, the ATO considers you to be an Australian resident for tax purposes if:

- You have always lived in Australia or you have come to Australia to live.

- You have been in Australia for more than half of the income year (unless your usual home is overseas and you do not intend to live in Australia – for example, you are a working holidaymaker).

- Or you are an overseas student enrolled in a course of study for more than six months' duration.

Therefore the majority of you will be considered by the tax office as an Australian Resident for tax purposes with the exception of those holding Working Holiday Visas. It is worth noting that the measures that the ATO uses to determine your residency status are not the same as those used by the Department of Immigration and Multicultural and Indigenous Affairs (DIMIA).

(For current tax rates refer to www.ato.gov.au/individuals)

Tax returns

www.ato.gov.au

As previously mentioned, most working holidaymakers are tourists or travellers visiting Australia and are not Australian residents for tax purposes. However, anyone who has been paid a salary or wages in Australia is encouraged to lodge an income tax return.

The Australian tax year ends on 30 June. You should lodge your tax return by 31 October, unless you have been granted an extension to lodge until a later date. You will have to pay more tax if you didn't pay enough while you were working. If too much tax was withheld from your pay, you will get a refund.

Brit tip

If you are leaving Australia before the end of the tax year, contact the ATO to see if you can lodge a return before you leave as you may be due some tax back which will send you on your travels with some extra money in your pocket.

Etax

You can prepare your tax return online via the ATO's website. You will need to wait for your employer to provide you with your end of year tax summary which should be available to you early in July. The procedure is very straightforward and allows you to calculate how much tax you should expect to receive back or how much you will need to pay. Once submitted your return should be processed within three weeks.

GST

The Australian GST is a Goods and Services Tax of 10% added to the price of most goods and services purchased in Australia. Usually GST has already been added to most products prior to your purchase (the amount on the clothes tag should include GST and the same with supermarket food etc) but it is worth keeping an eye out for as it can push the cost of goods and services up considerably.

SUPERANNUATION

Also known as super, this is a compulsory savings programme to make sure that when Australians reach retirement age they have some money to live on, and is the equivalent of our national insurance. Any employer you work for on a permanent basis must by law contribute to your super fund – the current minimum that they can pay is 9% of your salary. You do not need permanent residency to be entitled to this.

Most companies are affiliated with a fund manager, which is sometimes the simplest option; however, you do have a choice and can shop around for a plan that suits you. Should you change employers then you may have the choice of staying in your existing fund or rolling over to another fund.

Should you return to the UK

If you entered Australia on an eligible temporary resident visa and later permanently leave Australia then you can claim any superannuation you have accumulated, as you have no intention of retiring in the country. The payment will be subject to withholding tax and you can only claim your superannuation after you have had your visa cancelled and permanently departed from Australia (and can prove this).

You need to ask the Department of Immigration and Multicultural and Indigenous Affairs (DIMIA) to cancel the temporary resident's visa – for further information refer to www.imi.gov.au. It is worth noting that when you cancel your visa any member of your family who only holds a visa solely because you do will also automatically have theirs cancelled.

You will also need to complete a number of forms and provide detailed documentation as specified by your fund provider. Once the paperwork has been completed you can expect to have your money released (minus taxes) within 28 days.

Brit tip

When undergoing your job search, you should check if the salary that is advertised or that you are negotiating includes superannuation. If the figure being discussed does include the 9% contribution to your super then this could be inflating the real salary amount considerably. To gain a true reflection of your salary ask for the amount without super. This will really show what you will be earning, as you never see any of the superannuation money as it is deducted automatically from your wages along with tax.

BANKING AND FINANCE

Soon after your arrival in Australia you will find it necessary to open a bank account. As in the UK, there are many financial institutions to choose from. The most commonly found ones are:

- ANZ Bank – www.anz.com.au

- Westpac Bank – www.westpac.com.au

- Commonwealth Bank – www.commbank.com.au

- National Australia Bank – www.national.com.au

- St George – www.stgeorge.com.au

You will also recognise familiar institutions including HSBC and Citibank; however, you will still need to open a new Australian account providing the relevant documents. There are a lot of similarities between the leading banks but all of their rates do vary so it is worth shopping around to find the most appropriate one for your needs.

Can I open an account from the UK?

Some Australian banks do have a presence in the UK. Those that do will offer migrant services which should enable you to set up a bank account ahead of your arrival in Australia.

One such bank is the Commonwealth. Contact the London branch who will advise you if they can help: www.migrantbanking.co.uk

What do I need to open a bank account?

When opening an account you will need as much proof of identity as possible, including your passport.

Most financial institutions work on a points system to ensure the identification of a person seeking to open a bank account. Your chosen bank will explain the system when you open the account. It's a good idea to ring them first so you don't waste your time and you can bring the necessary documentation.

Current points (as of 2005)

You need to achieve 100 points to open an account.

Birth certificate		
Passport		
Citizenship certificate	**70 points**	You can only get points for one item in this section
Driving licence	**40 points**	These cards must have a photograph or signature

Any card on which your name appears:
Medicare card
Credit card (only one per institution)
Store account card
Library card
Union card   **25 points**

Documents on which your name and address appear:
Car registration
Utility bills   **25 points**

Types of accounts

Most accounts are deposit accounts. These include accounts such as term deposits, savings accounts, cheque accounts, and cash management accounts.

Overdrafts

Overdrafts are not offered by most Australian banks for deposit accounts. They are not considered as a standard facility, which might come to a shock to most Brits who live on theirs! Should you require one you will need to negotiate with your bank which may well impose strict regulations on this facility. If you are not fortunate enough to be granted one then you run the risk of being charged $30 plus every time you go into the red.

It is worth mentioning that Australian banks charge more for their services than British banks so do familiarise yourself with the small print when choosing with whom to bank.

Credit

Gaining credit can also be problematic for non-residents. It is unlikely that any financial institution will offer this facility as a matter of course and it may take you some time to gain a decent enough credit rating to secure a credit card or loan – even if you are a high earner. This may come as a surprise to many Brits who have been used to gaining credit very easily in the UK. It also can be somewhat frustrating as many of the online facilities (such as internet ticket booking for entertainment, sport, cinema etc) will not accept British cards.

> **Brit tip**
>
> Virgin have launched their credit card in Australia, which offers extremely competitive rates and is more flexible for non-residents than other banks'.

Are there notable differences between Australian and British banking facilities?

EFTPOS (Electronic Funds Transfer at Point Of Sale) is the Australian alternative to our SWITCH system. When you open an account you will be given an EFTPOS card, which you can use as payment around Australia. It is a bank card that is swiped through a small machine as you would expect but it *does not* require a signature – instead the card holder enters his/her pin number and EFTPOS simply transfers the value approved from the selected account (either cheque or savings) into the account held by the merchant.

Loans and mortgages

Personal loans and mortgages can be complicated for people with temporary residence in Australia; however, there are some specialist moneylenders who will assist non-residents in gaining a competitive home loan. These options can be explored in detail when you have established yourselves there. It is also important to know that investment in the Australian property market generally requires pre-approval from the Foreign Investment Review Board. It is the responsibility of the purchaser to inquire if any approval is required. If you are thinking about buying a property immediately or soon after arrival in Australia I strongly suggest that you make detailed enquiries about feasibility and requirements prior to leaving the UK.

For further information about mortgages in Australia refer to www.yourmortgage.com.au

Brit tip

- The majority of Australian banks do not yet open at the weekends so check your branch's opening hours and where possible opt for telephone/internet banking for your convenience.

- If you intend to send money back to the UK regularly, do compare the various banks' charges for doing this as just one transaction of this type can cost up to $50 (not to mention incurring costs in the UK for receiving funds).

- Nearly all the banks only allow customers a certain number of free transactions per month (either ATM or EFTPOS) therefore do look out for this when researching accounts as you could end up paying a lot of hidden monthly charges.

• One way of avoiding additional transaction charges is to get cash back when using your EFTPOS card – many retailers including supermarkets and some bottleshops offer this facility. This is particularly useful in the Outback where there are very few ATMs.

6
The Australian Healthcare System

MEDICARE

What is Medicare?

Medicare is Australia's public health care system. It is a high quality system which provides eligible people with access to free treatment as a public (Medicare) patient in a public hospital, as well as free or subsidised treatment on a private basis by doctors (both general practitioners and specialists). Eligibility for Medicare also gives access to the Pharmaceutical Benefits Scheme (PBS) which covers most prescription pharmaceuticals provided by pharmacies.

Am I eligible for it?

Medicare eligibility is generally restricted to people living permanently in Australia; however, there are some exceptions.

Australia has Reciprocal Health Care Agreements with eight countries including the UK and Ireland (the others being New Zealand, the Netherlands, Sweden, Finland, Italy and Malta). Under these agreements, residents of these countries have restricted access to Medicare while visiting Australia. It is worth noting that each of these agreements is different from the others so if you are from another country you will need to check out your entitlements.

What does Medicare cover?

These agreements give visitors from these countries access to Medicare for the treatment of an illness or injury which occurs during their stay, and which requires treatment before returning home (that is, these agreements cover immediately necessary medical treatment). The agreements do not allow for visitors to access Medicare or the Pharmaceutical Benefits Scheme where the treatment is not immediately necessary. Prearranged and elective treatment is not covered.

What doesn't Medicare cover?

The agreements do not cover all health services. Some services not covered under the agreements are:

- ambulance cover

- dental care

- medical evacuation to your home country

- treatment in private hospitals, or as a private patient in a public hospital

- treatment that is not immediately necessary

- elective treatment

- treatment that has been pre-arranged before arrival in Australia.

Do I pay to see a doctor or for prescriptions?

Yes to both. Shortly after you arrive in Australia I suggest that you register with a local doctor (you can find one by looking in the *Yellow Pages* or asking locals in your area).

Each time you have an appointment with your doctor you will be charged a fee depending on how much of their time you have taken. Currently, this ranges between $55 and $110. These are standard fees which most people pay up front unless other arrangements have been made with the surgery. You will then be given a receipt(s), which you can take to a Medicare centre where you can claim a proportion back.

Enrolling in Medicare

If you know you are eligible for Medicare you will need to go to a Medicare office to enrol, taking your passport and any additional ID or proof of visa status. You can either telephone 132 011 (local call cost if calling from within Australia) or visit a Medicare office to confirm what documentation you will need to provide in order to enrol in Medicare. Once you have completed the paperwork, and if you are eligible, you will be given a Medicare number instantly, which will be followed by a Medicare Card.

www.medicare.gov.au

> **Brit tip**
>
> Enrol with Medicare as soon as is convenient after arrival in Australia. You never know when you will need it and not having it in place can cause problems should you require medical treatment.

What happens if I need to go to hospital or accident and emergency?

Obviously you should not hesitate to seek immediate medical assistance either by calling 000 (the countrywide number for all emergency services in Australia) for an ambulance or by getting yourself to any of the numerous local hospitals. You should inform hospital staff that you wish to be treated as a Medicare public patient under a Reciprocal Health Care Agreement. You may be required to produce evidence of your eligibility (ie your passport with visa stamp or Medicare card) either at the time of your visit or a later date.

PRIVATE HEALTHCARE

Can I opt for private healthcare?

There is a wide range of private healthcare options available across Australia, which are well worth inquiring about to ensure you receive the highest care available without the waiting lists associated with public health services.

www.health.gov.au is the government run health website which provides valuable information about healthcare across Australia, including research on the best private funds to join, enabling people to make informed choices.

Brit tip

- If you need a prescription urgently or can't get a doctor's appointment with your own surgery you can drop in at any medical centre of which there are many in the larger cities. You will have to wait to be seen, but a doctor will see you regardless of whether or not you have an appointment.

- Word of mouth is a good way to find a doctor or dentist so do ask around for recommendations.

- You may initially begrudge paying to see a doctor, but the benefits far outweigh the disadvantages as you are able to see doctors at short notice and the level of care is high. You do also get back a large proportion of what you pay out.

DENTAL SERVICES

Medicare does not cover dental work in Australia. Therefore you will need to find a dentist local to your area and should expect to pay for any work needed, which of course varies enormously depending on what you need to have done. You can find dentists nationwide across Australia and as with anywhere, professional levels vary. Word of mouth is a good way of ensuring that you join a reputable dental surgery. Check for ads in your local paper, or search the *Yellow Pages* online to find a suitable dentist in your area.

Some private health funds do cover dental work, so if you opt to join one check to see what is covered under your plan.

7
Education and Childcare

Australia is a refreshingly child-friendly place to live and a wonderful place to raise a family. The abundance of parks and excellent outdoor activities and facilities ensure that children grow up enjoying the outdoors and all it has to offer.

Australia ranks fifth as having the most effective education system among the world's richest countries, according to a United Nations study in 2002. South Korea leads the ranking ahead of Japan, Finland, Canada and Australia, with Britain ranked seventh, New Zealand equal tenth and the United States 18th among the 24 nations.

EDUCATION

The Australian education system is different from the UK's and varies slightly from State to State, and the ages for each level of education may vary by a year or two. Schooling is compulsory for students in most States and Territories until the age of 15. Although students are able to leave at that time, most students do not leave until they complete their Year 10 qualification, with many students staying on to complete their Year 12 studies.

There are cost implications for children of non-residents which can run to thousands of dollars a year per child – please refer to further information in the city sections.

School hours

State primary and high schools generally run from 9am to 3pm, Monday to Friday, except for public holidays and school holidays. Individual schools and States may set slightly different starting and finishing times.

Term dates

The Aussie school year begins in February and is divided into four terms. As in the UK, schools have many holidays throughout the year including Easter, summer, Christmas, etc. You will need to confirm with your local school which ones are applicable as they vary throughout the country.

GUIDE TO THE AUSSIE EDUCATION SYSTEM

Most public schools (State government) are mixed sex and multicultural.

Pre-school

For youngsters aged around 4–6 years. Education is basic and skills-based, involving reading, structured play, painting, etc.

Primary school

For children aged 6 to around 12 starting at kindergarten and running from years 1 to 6. This is where all the basic subjects are taught including maths, English, geography, science etc. Some introductory foreign languages may be taught and a growing emphasis is placed on sport.

High school

In most States this is six years long (years 7 to 12), but in some (eg the Australian Capital State), it is only four years long, with the final two years being completed in college. High school students should have learnt all the subjects to basic adult levels or above by the end of Year 10 when they achieve the School Certificate, which is an educational credential. They then go on to years 11 and 12 where they study for their Higher School Certificate.

Qualifications

The Higher School Certificate is more commonly referred to as the HSC. Students must have achieved their School Certificate or equivalent in order to be able to study for their HSC and enter Year 11 (called Preliminary). Students must pass various assessments that year in order to be able to move on to Year 12 (HSC). The only compulsory subject is English and all other subjects are electives that vary from school to school. Assessment is made up of 50% internal school assessment and 50% external HSC examination assessment.

How to enrol your child in school

When you enrol your child in any school you will need to take proof of their date of birth, such as the child's birth certificate, passport or visa. Contact the school direct to get the necessary forms.

Fees

Non-residents will have to pay for their children's school. Fees vary depending on whether you choose to send your kids to a state or private school and are generally in excess of $4,500 per child, per year. Each of the States has different guidelines and charges in place – refer to the education section of the chapter on the State to which you are considering moving for further information.

DIFFERENCES BETWEEN UK AND AUSTRALIA

In Australia you will find that children are encouraged to take more responsibility for their own learning by being encouraged to participate and ask questions. Smaller classes help with children's development.

A greater emphasis is also placed on behaviour rather than academic achievement at younger ages and social skills are proactively taught. Sport and outdoor activities are also considered to play a crucial role in children's schooling.

Most schools are eager for parental involvement and wish to help newcomers, which is welcome news for migrants. Parent teacher associations play crucial roles in raising funds for many school needs but parents are also allowed a say in what is taught and done at the school.

PUBLIC V PRIVATE

You can choose to have your children educated in public (State government) or private (independent) schools throughout the country.

Private or independent schools have their own fee structure and are generally either exclusively all boy or all girl schools.

FURTHER EDUCATION

The University Admission Index (UAI)

If students wish to be considered for admission to university they must choose a combination of HSC subjects that are acceptable for university entry and must apply for a UAI (University Admission Index). The UAI is a calculated rank, which is based on ten units of Board Developed Courses and involves a combination of the scaled HSC exam mark and the moderated assessment marks.

Vocational Education and Training (VET) courses

Vocational Education and Training courses are offered as part of the Higher School Certificate.

As well as general academic subjects high schools also provide VET courses in Years 11 and 12. These courses are in a diverse range of subjects such as IT and retail and can be included on a UAI programme of study if the external exam is undertaken at the end of Year 12. The aim of these courses is to enable students to study subjects which are relevant to industry needs and have clear links to post-school destinations. These courses allow students to gain both Higher School Certificate qualifications and accreditation with industry and the workplace as part of the Australian Qualifications Framework (AQF).

For further information on HSC, VET and further education refer to www.thegoodguides.com.au

University

There are approximately 40 Australian universities catering for students aged 19+. They are both teaching and research institutions and cover the full range of academic and professional disciplines leading to many different qualifications.

The number of overseas students in Australian institutions continues to grow. More than 180,000 international students study there. Australia has the third largest number of international students in the English-speaking world behind the USA and the United Kingdom, but in many countries Australia is the students' first choice for international study.

The tuition fees and living costs to study in Australia compare well with most other countries, with quality tuition being more affordable when studying in Australia than in the United Kingdom or the USA.

TAFE

TAFE (Technical and Further Education) is another option instead of university. It is effectively a trade school, offering diplomas in many relevant subjects.

CHILDCARE

Average costs of a good quality day care centre are $80 per child per day (0-5 years old).

Brit tip

Check out the care for kids website www.careforkids.com.au for comprehensive information about child care resources in Australia, including details of au pairs, nannies and local child care facilities.

8
Renting Your Australian Home

AN OVERVIEW OF THE CURRENT RENTAL MARKET

The prices below will give you an idea of the average rental costs for properties of each type – obviously homes can be found in the upper and lower scale of these depending on size, location etc. (Prices accurate at time of writing: May 2005.)

Rental prices per month						
1 bed apartment (unfurnished) in a decent suburb						
Sydney	Melbourne	Brisbane	Perth	Adelaide	Canberra	Tasmania*
$270	$230	$200	$200	$190	$215	$160
2 bed apartment (unfurnished) in a decent suburb						
Sydney	Melbourne	Brisbane	Perth	Adelaide	Canberra	Tasmania*
$400	$375	$300	$325	$300	$325	$225
3 bedroom house (unfurnished) in a decent suburb						
Sydney	Melbourne	Brisbane	Perth	Adelaide	Canberra	Tasmania*
$600	$500	$475	$475	$450	$450	$350

*Tasmania prices based on the capital, Hobart

CHOOSING WHERE TO LIVE

Even if you have visited Australia before, you may not be familiar with all the cities and their suburbs. So how do you decide where to live? I suggest that you take some time prior to your arrival in the country to do some research and have a good think about what factors are likely to influence your decisions.

For example, are you restricted by budget? How important is lifestyle to you? Is location the most important factor or is it a mix or all three and more?

Finding a location that suits your new Australian lifestyle is important – especially if you are seeking a change in lifestyle, which is one of the main reasons that people leave the UK to live and work in Oz.

Things to consider:

- Do you want to live near to a beach? (It is a long way to come to live in the city!)
- Do you want an apartment or a house?
- Commuting times.
- Budget.
- Proximity to schools.
- Childcare accessibility.

How to research areas of interest

This useful on-line guide provides detailed information about rental and house prices in every area of Australia:
www.domain.com.au/Public/SuburbReport.aspx

Brit tip

The Suburb Snapshot gives average prices for houses and units (the Australian name for flats or apartments) over a 12-month period. It also gives a breakdown of suburb population, public transport, demographics and more.

HOW TO START YOUR SEARCH FOR A RENTAL PROPERTY

Property agents

There are numerous real estate agents who can help you with your search for a home, and most of the large companies have branches in every major city and its suburbs. There are many ways of locating them. If you already know the areas you are keen on you can look up a list of agents in that area from the *Yellow Pages* (either online at www.yellowpages.com.au or locally dial 12451) and call them to find out what they have available. Alternatively you can visit the estate agents in person and pick up their current rentals lists, which are usually updated weekly and provide times and dates that the properties are available to view.

Online

The internet is a valuable resource when searching for a property. All of the leading real estate agents have websites which enable you to search the suburbs you are interested in and allow you to specify your requirements. These should provide you with a list of suitable properties which you can arrange to either visit by appointment or view at 'open inspection'. This is the route most real estate agents take to show their properties to prospective tenants and simply means that at a certain time and date properties are open for a short time for everyone to inspect. You should be prepared to fit in around their timings and, as most do not work on Sundays, this may well involve you scheduling many viewings back to back on Saturdays – particularly in the mornings. The homes are usually open for 15-minute periods, and agents will not wait for you should you be running late, therefore it is crucial that you are organised and know where you are going.

Useful real estate sites

These sites are not restricted to any real estate agent and offer the most comprehensive way to establish the current rental market for prices and availability. You can also register with them to receive email updates when properties meeting your requirements are placed on the site, ensuring that you are always at the front of the queue and well informed.

www.domain.com.au

www.rent-a-home.com.au

www.realestate.com.au

A word of warning

The internet is a useful tool to research property from overseas but can be misleading. Prior to leaving the UK we spent many a rainy London night searching the Sydney rental market for our dream home and were captivated by endless images of sunny apartments with ocean views and large outdoor entertaining areas (perfect for all the 'barbies' we were going to have!). Although this provided us with a good idea of how to actually go about finding somewhere to live when on the ground and an overview of the different suburbs, all of the beautiful images and descriptions actually gave us a false idea of what we could get for our money. This is due to the fact that when viewing properties on-line from the UK you cannot fail to convert the rental prices back in to pounds.

This gives you an unrealistic view of what it will actually cost you as you will not be earning pounds but Aussie dollars and your wages are unlikely to provide you with the income you are used to.

Brit tip

• Do use the internet to research areas you might be interested in – make a list of your favourites to explore on arrival.

• Do *not* use the internet to calculate your rental costs for the next six months as it will not truly reflect the cost of living when you are working there and earning dollars.

• Do use the internet to help ascertain what you require from a home and suburb.

Local publications

These can be useful ways to research the current property market in the area(s) you are considering living in. Ask your local newsagent which one is available in your area – they will usually stock them for free.

Brit tip

Check what day of the week the guides come out and pick them up early that day. All the best properties are snapped up instantly so ensure that you're at least in with a fighting chance by checking listings as quickly as possible.

ONCE YOU HAVE FOUND SOMEWHERE

Real estate agents work on a first come first served basis. During 'open inspections', or indeed by private appointment, you have the following opportunities.

Placing a deposit

Should you be enamoured by a property and want to have the best chance of securing a lease on it, you should immediately tell the agent that you would like to place a deposit on it. This should effectively take it off the market immediately and prevent them from showing it to any other potential tenants. This is a key tactic if you are attending a popular viewing where one or more applications for tenancy may be lodged. You will then need to fill in an application form (either joint or single) that will be submitted to the owner.

Taking an application form

Should you like a property but have more to see and wish to make a more informed decision, you can take an application form from the agent and apply later. Of course you do run the risk that a deposit or application may have been taken by the time you submit yours, but you should never feel pressured into making this sort of decision unless you are completely confident of your choice.

THE APPLICATION PROCESS

A tenancy application form has to be filled in regardless of whether you have placed a deposit on the required property or not. The forms vary from company to company but are generally straightforward and require you to give all the usual personal information. However, if you have only just arrived in the country and are not yet employed this may complicate matters as your landlord will want proof that you are who you say you are and can pay the rent.

Brit tip

- If you are not yet employed, be prepared to pay three months upfront (especially if you are leasing a property with high rent) and also a bond. Your landlord may require this if you have no Australian financial references to rely on.

- Be ready to supply references from the UK both professionally and personally – email addresses for them will help speed up your application process.

LEASE TERMS AND CONDITIONS

You should check the proposed length of lease on the property with the real estate agent or landlord at the viewing stage. The minimum lease is usually six months with the average being twelve. Leases in Australia are hard to break and it is not a case of simply giving notice should you want to move out prior to the end of your contract. There could be considerable financial implications in lease breaking so do consider your terms carefully.

Brit tip

- When attending viewings it is wise to carry enough cash or a cheque book so that you are in a position to place a deposit.

- Do try haggling over the rental price. Landlords and letting agents would prefer to let their property for a lower rent than be empty for any period of time.

- Take the minimum lease possible (usually six months) if you have not yet secured a job or if you are not 100% sure of the area. This will allow you to move on should things not work out as planned – remember you can always renew your lease should you want to stay.

- Where possible, rent a property that has air conditioning. The summer months are incredibly hot (especially by British standards) and balmy evening temperatures often lead to restless nights. Although the winters are mild, temperatures drop considerably in the evenings and once you are acclimatised you may well be cold. Air conditioners can usually be reversed to release warm air.

Private leasing

You can cut out agents by dealing with landlords directly. Some homeowners prefer not to pay the rather significant management and services charges the agents demand and advertise their homes on a website or in local publications. You must weigh up the pros and cons of doing this to decide if this might be an option for you.

WHAT TO EXPECT WHEN RENTING A PROPERTY

Bonds

All letting agents will require you to place a rental bond as a form of security against any potential breaches of the agreement or breakages. The amount varies but you should expect to pay at least four weeks' rent.

During the tenancy, your bond is held by Renting and Strata Services, not by the agent. Once your tenancy comes to an end and after the property has been inspected, a Claim for Refund of Bond Money form should be filled out by the landlord or agent and given to the tenant to sign. Should there be any issues over deductions from the bond for carpet cleaning, damages etc they will be raised before the claim for refund of bond money is submitted.

Condition report

Before you move in, the agent will inspect the property and fill out a condition report. You will be given a copy of this and it is crucial that you check this to be a realistic account of what condition the premises are in. This report may be the only piece of evidence should there be any disputes at the end of the tenancy with regards to its condition.

Services

Unless stated otherwise to you, landlords are usually responsible for paying all service charges for water and sewerage issued by the local water supply authority.

Furnished or unfurnished

The majority of rental homes in Sydney and NSW are offered completely unfurnished. This is a huge point of difference between renting in the UK and in Australia. The chances are that you will need to purchase or rent everything you need for your home, including fridge, freezer, pots and pans, beds, sofas, not to mention all of your electrical equipment. This is a huge expense to incur as soon as you arrive but might unfortunately be a necessity. For places to shop and ways to save you considerable amounts of money please refer to Chapter 10.

WHEN YOU FIRST ARRIVE

Unless you are relocating with your company or moving in with family or friends, it's unlikely that you will have an apartment already set up and ready to move into, so you may need somewhere to stay in the interim period. There are plenty of hotels you can check into which range from inexpensive to top of the market. The following sites offer good rates:

www.wotif.com.au

www.needitnow.com.au

Serviced apartments

Serviced apartments offer a wonderful alternative to hotels for many reasons. They allow you the freedom to cater for yourself and do as you please whilst making less of a dent in your savings. If you are unsure of the properties' locations then do some research and make sure they are convenient for your needs. The following websites cover a range of properties, from private short-term rental homes to longer-term serviced apartments offering extra facilities including gym, pool and internet access.

www.apartmentservice.com.au

www.medinaapartments.com.au

House sharing

If you would prefer to share your home with other people then there are some wonderful properties out there and some great sites dedicated to matching people. If you arrive on your own this can be a useful way of starting life out in Australia, save you lots of money and be a good way of meeting people. If you are interested in sharing then the following sites can help:

www.flatmatefinders.com.au

www.flatmates.com.au

Brit tip

- If you are not keen on spending lots of money immediately on big household items or furniture then you may choose to rent the majority of your items. Just about everything you may need for your home can be hired instead of purchased. This can be a really good option, and cost effective in the short term, until you are confident of your plans. In general, the minimum rental period is one month and they will offer discounts for package deals. Rental items include: beds, fridges, televisions, washing machines, sofas, dining room tables. You can even rent lamps and bedding should you so desire. Items will be delivered to you at your convenience.

For furniture throughout the home and outdoors:

- PABS: www.pabs.com.au

For electrical equipment and smaller household items

- Rentacentre: www.rentacentre.com.au

USEFUL TERMINOLOGY

- **Units** – you will see a lot of 'units' available for lease. This is an Australian term for an apartment or flat.

- **Deck** – if the property is listed as having a deck, this refers to an outside space which is usually wooden. Units can have decks on either a balcony or roof terrace, as can houses with courtyards.

- **Body corporate** – this term is generally only used in conjunction with apartments or units. It refers to a corporation of the owners of units within a building who have formed a self-elected council for the management of the building and common areas. For example, if you are renting a home and want to install cable or satellite you may not only have to ask permission from the landlord and or letting agent, you may need permission from the body corporate for the building as well.

9
Utilities

As in the UK there are many companies providing similar services. Competition between businesses in Australia is less fierce than in the UK and it is a well known fact that certain companies have a monopoly in their markets. However, this does not mean that as a consumer you don't have options, so do shop around to ensure you are getting the most competitive deal and best service available.

TELECOMMUNICATIONS

Landlines

When you have found a property to move into, or even at the viewing stage, you should check whether there is a phone line already in place, otherwise you may have to arrange for one to be installed which is an additional expense that you could do without. If your home already has a phone connection (as will be the case for most rental homes) you should expect to pay a one-off connection charge of approximately $60 to your chosen service provider.

What to expect

Most bills are issued on a monthly basis as opposed to quarterly. When you choose your provider they will ask you to select a monthly plan that is appropriate to your personal needs. There are plenty of options to suit all requirements and they vary in cost depending on what kind of calls you intend to make. International calls are very reasonable between landlines and won't make a huge dent in your pocket.

Main service providers

Optus – www.optus.com.au

Telstra – www.telstra.com.au

Brit tip

- By far the cheapest way to make international calls is by purchasing an international phone card. These allow you to call from any phone line (all landlines and even mobiles) for hugely discounted rates above and beyond what the main phone providers can offer. The phone cards were designed primarily with the backpacker in mind; however, many people use them to keep their phone bills low. The Hello card is a popular option as it is currently the cheapest way of calling the UK – a ten dollar card will give you a whopping four hours' call time. You can also use these cards when travelling around Australia and they make a cheap alternative to hotel phones and international mobile charges. Your newsagent will be able to advise on which card best suits your particular needs.

- Remember the time difference otherwise your call home may not prove to be popular! Australia is ahead by 8–11 hours depending whereabouts in the country you are and at what time of the year and whether it is daylight saving or not. A rule of thumb guide is that morning UK time is evening in Australia and vice versa.

Mobiles

If you arrive in the country with a British mobile still connected you may well decide for financial reasons and convenience to get hooked up locally. There are phone shops everywhere so you won't find it difficult to become mobile quickly. You should note that in Australia, most mobile phone providers do like to lock customers into longer contracts than in the UK – most offering two years as the standard with hefty financial penalties for early termination. If you don't arrive with a visa proving that you are entitled to be in the country for the length of the contract then you may have to start with a pay-as-you-go phone package. These are a cheap and efficient option, costing only around $25 – $40 to obtain a sim card and most companies will give you this back as phone credit. It really does pay to shop around, to take advantage of promotions and specials and make sure that you check the small print.

You should be aware that network coverage varies enormously in Australia, so do ask advice about the signal strength in your area and others of importance to you.

The main providers are: Telstra, Optus, Orange, Virgin Mobile, Vodafone, 3 and Austar.

Brit tip

- Purchase a pay-as-you-go mobile if you do not want to commit to lengthy contracts immediately on arrival. You can always change over when you are sure of your plans.

- If you intend to spend considerable time in the bush or off the beaten track then it is wise to look into obtaining a CDMA (code division multiple access) phone as this is the only way to ensure that you will get coverage in many of the non-urban and inland areas.

Internet

The number of Australian households with access to the internet continues to increase and if you are looking to have internet access at home then there is a range of options open to you.

There are dial up, broadband and ADSL options as you would expect and the two largest providers, Telstra and Optus, both offer many packages within their services. As this is a growth industry other companies are constantly updating their services in order to compete.

Main service providers:

www.bigpond.com (Telstra)

www.optusnet.com.au

www.iprimus.com.au

www.dodo.com.au

Again, do shop around for both prices and flexibility on your contract as they do try to lock you in for lengthy minimums which are not easy to get out of.

> **Brit tip**
>
> There are financial benefits to choosing the same supplier for both your home phone and internet services – do discuss this at the sales stage. Further reductions may apply if you also subscribe to their pay TV services.

WATER

If you are renting a property then in most cases your landlord will be liable for your water charges and there should be no need for you to contact the water company. Should this not be the case then ask your letting agent to give you details of the provider in your area as different companies service each of the states in Australia.

GAS AND ELECTRICITY

Energy Australia is one of the country's largest and oldest suppliers of gas and electricity. If you need to connect to both then you can do so via this company. Customers are usually billed quarterly.

www.energy.com.au

A USEFUL SHORTCUT

Utilityone is a company that will connect your telephone, electricity, gas and water utilities (where applicable) on your behalf at no extra cost and with no extra contracts involved. They are paid a fee by the provider for streamlining the process and delivering information to them electronically, saving them the normal costs (call centres, etc) which is why they can offer this service to you free. Contact them prior to moving into your property and they will help you with all your requirements, saving both time and hassle.

www.utilityone.com.au

TELEVISION

There are five free to air channels in Australia. Channels 7, 9 and 10 are commercial networks that can be compared with our ITV, and Channel 4 and 5 showing a blend of news, current affairs, soaps, movies, sport and reality TV shows.

SBS is a multicultural and multilingual service that provides a mix of quality Australian and international programmes. The fifth free to air channel is the ABC which is Australia's only national, non-commercial broadcaster. The ABC is considered an important part of Australia's cultural heritage, fostering the arts and reflecting the nation's cultural diversity in much the same way that the BBC does in the UK. It is funded by the government out of public taxes. You should be able to receive all of these channels free by connecting your television aerial; however, there may be a variation in picture quality depending on where you live.

Pay TV

In addition to the free to air channels you can opt to subscribe to Foxtel or Austar, which are Australia's version of Sky, offering consumers a wide variety of channels including movies, sport, entertainment, news etc. Both offer the same programming but service different areas of the country.

- www.austar.com.au
- www.foxtel.com.au

10
Shopping Guide – How to Save Time and Money

FURNISHING YOUR HOME

Unless you have found a very reasonably priced furnished home (which are few and far between) or are shipping all your belongings from the UK (enormously expensive unless of course your company is paying for your relocation), then chances are that you will need to purchase the majority of your furniture and home appliances. Potentially this will make a huge dent in your savings, and if you do not have a job to go to immediately you may be reluctant to spend a lot of money unnecessarily. You can save yourself hundreds of dollars just by knowing where to shop.

If you are looking to purchase new items but at good prices then there are a few places that can save you both time and money.

Stores to know about

For crockery, cutlery, towels and all the little bits and pieces that you might need such as bins, pots and pans etc, K-mart is hard to beat for value and prides itself on guaranteeing its customers the lowest prices. Two other stores offering fantastic value on an enormous range of everyday household items and clothing (amongst other things) are Target and Big W. All have stores in major towns and cities and are hugely popular in Australia.

For those with more generous budgets Bayswiss stocks a beautiful range of furniture and accessories including vases, candles, crockery and cushions. Their stores have an upmarket feel to them but are still affordable and they have fabulous sales throughout the year. Some of their stores also have delis with wonderful foods, which you can eat in or take away.

For opening hours or to locate a store refer to:

www.kmart.com.au

www.target.com.au

www.bigw.com.au

www.bayswiss.com.au

If you are a DIY enthusiast or want outdoor furniture for your new home, trying Bunnings Warehouse which is the Aussie equivalent of B&Q and Homebase.

www.bunnings.com.au

ELECTRICALS

There is a wide range of stores stocking electrical goods that have branches nationwide including Bing Lee, Dick Smith and The Good Guys. All stock a wide range of goods for the home including TVs, irons, fridges, computers etc. Prices will range so do shop around.

The Electric Discounter aims to offer the most competitive deals across Australia and it is worth checking out their website to see if they can offer you savings.

www.theelectricdiscounter.com.au

Brit tip

Do haggle if you are paying in cash or in bulk. Australian retailers are willing to slash prices if it will secure a sale.

SUPERMARKETS

Australia's two main supermarkets, Coles and Woolworths, are also good places to pick up cheap and cheerful household items and offer both convenience and value. Within the cities there are smaller metro stores offering a more limited range but there's sure to be a store close by. You can also shop on-line for items for delivery. Of course they also cater for all your grocery needs.

Whilst the supermarkets are great for stocking up on store cupboard items, it's worth noting that in Australia most people shop daily in order to fully benefit from the wonderfully fresh produce on offer. There is an abundance of quality butchers, fishmongers, bakers, fruit and vegetable stores and delicatessens, which are frequented by people on their way home. They are well priced and convenient for both cooking and entertaining, or for picking up dinner to share with friends in the park, which is common in the summer months.

www.coles.com.au

www.woolworths.com.au

DEPARTMENT STORES

David Jones and Myer are the main two department stores in Australia, and both offer consumers a wide variety of high quality products including men's and women's clothing, cosmetics, jewellery, home furnishings, etc. David Jones is more traditional in feel and can be compared with John Lewis in their commitment to ensuring consumers the best in service, value and range of products. In some David Jones stores you will also find the most wonderful food halls offering an incredible selection of exceptional fresh produce including meats, fish, cheeses, sea foods, deli items, cakes and pastries, not to mention a good selection of fine wines. The food halls are well worth a visit to pick up dinner on your way home or just to stop and have a quick bite to eat or even a glass of champagne at the oyster bar. To find a store near you or check product lines check out their website.

www.davidjones.com.au

www.myer.com.au

Myer has recently undergone an image and name change. Believe it or not until 2004 it was called Grace Bros, which of course was the name of a well known seventies British sitcom! Since its re-launch the brand has a more youthful feel to it and the stores reflect this, offering consumers a modern, broad range of items including everything you would expect a large department store to stock.

SECONDHAND

A great way of picking up bargains is to buy your household goods secondhand. This is a common way for migrants to furnish their homes as there is a constant flow of people in and out of the country therefore many people sell their goods on when they leave.

The most common ways to purchase used goods is via ads in the local newspapers, *The Trading Post* (see below) or garage sales. Of course ebay (www.ebay.com.au) is an increasingly popular way of buying and selling secondhand goods and is worth surfing for bargains.

The Trading Post

The Trading Post is a nationwide publication which offers a comprehensive range of new and used goods including cars, electrical, home furnishings and pets. It enables you to search by location and price and is a great place to pick up bargains.

www.tradingpost.com.au

Garage sales

These are an Aussie tradition and tend to take place over weekends. The term refers to when people sell items from their house either as part of a spring cleaning or moving home sale. You will regularly see signs displayed in local shops or newsagents with a time, date and address. People tend to get there early in order to pick up the best items at dirt-cheap prices.

Charity shops

Australian high streets would not be complete without a St Vinnies charity shop. They are generally of a good standard, selling secondhand clothes and items, and are worth popping into on a regular basis to see what gems are on offer.

PART 2
WORKING IN …

Melbourne

11
The Job Market in Australia

MANAGING YOUR EXPECTATIONS

If you are coming to Australia with the notion of furthering your career but do not have a job lined up or any contacts, I can't stress enough the importance of researching your chosen market prior to making the life-changing decision to relocate.

THE REALITIES

The chances are that you may well have to take a considerable pay cut and (or) take a position that could be considered a step back or two in your career ladder to order to gain some experience in the Australian markets. Therefore do ensure that this is something you are prepared to do ahead of your visa application. The country may be enormous but the job markets generally are on a much smaller scale than our large cities such as London and Manchester. This means that competition for some professional jobs (eg banking, marketing, law, etc) is fierce and Australian employers do reserve the right to exclude non-residents from applying for any job. As a nation the Aussies are passionately patriotic, and do like to promote from within as well, which limits opportunities for overseas workers even more.

In order to meet Australia's strict visa entry requirements, you might also have to consider living and working in rural areas where you may be able to meet local skills shortages. On the whole there is no shortage of workers in the metropolitan cities of Sydney, Perth and Melbourne therefore you might have to be flexible in location and consider moving to areas further afield such as Tasmania or regional South Australia.

Don't panic though, as the country's economy is strong and there are some fantastic opportunities available throughout the country for UK workers – you just have to find them!

As you would expect, there are no set rules as to how easily you'll find work in Australia, and it will depend on many factors, but the following may help you with your search for employment.

WHERE TO BEGIN

If you are seeking to permanently live and work in Australia then you must ensure that you are able to find work as the Australian government will *not* grant visas to migrants who cannot provide evidence that they can support themselves and their families.

It is therefore essential that you evaluate the current Australian job market to establish if your occupation is one that is currently in demand. Even if you enter the country on a temporary visa with the aim of finding work, it is an awfully long way to come to discover that the market you are looking for work in is in decline or flooded with applications from Australian residents.

Research is the key to you ensuring that you maximise all of the potential job opportunities that are available to you.

www.workplace.gov.au

AN OVERVIEW OF THE CURRENT JOB MARKET

The current situation

Australia is enjoying a booming economy with unemployment at its lowest for 20 years. It is a country full of opportunities for foreign workers. Savvy, skilled professionals should be able to forge wonderful careers here providing that they are realistic in their expectations. There is a variety of job opportunities across Australia, ranging from tradespersons to professionals and business executives. In fact, 2006/2007 is the best possible time for skilled Brits to look for work in Australia as labour analysts have predicted a dire skills shortage in Australia over the next ten years as the country's ageing population faces retirement.

In August 2005, the Australian government announced details of a large-scale recruitment programme aimed directly at skilled British labour, which is fantastic news for job seekers. This new recruitment drive is reminiscent of the 'Ten Pound Pom' campaigns of the 1950s and 1960s and is an indication of how in demand skilled British workers are across the country.

In particular, the government hopes to attract skilled British migrants to the country's various regional States under recently relaxed regulations. The government has expanded its 2006 migration programme to include 20,000 extra visas, which is a significant increase on previous years.

On announcing the 2005-06 Migration (non-Humanitarian) Programme, the Minister for Immigration and Multicultural and Indigenous Affairs, Senator Amanda Vanstone commented, 'Migrants are playing a vital role in helping to address the critical skill shortages felt by employers in local communities across Australia'.

Employment

In the 12 months to May 2006, the Australian labour market experienced solid growth and total employment increased by an estimated 122,600 persons (1.2%). All States and Territories experienced increases, with Western Australia seeing the strongest employment growth at 2.5% (source: Australian Labour Market Update July 2006).

GROWTH AND DECLINE AREAS

Australia is somewhat behind its European counterparts from a technological point of view and the country is desperately trying to find skilled IT workers to help take the country forward. People with information technology skills are in very high demand and according to estimates from the Australian Information Industry Association the total number of job vacancies in the IT sector in Australia is estimated to be around 30,000 (correct in 2005).

This is not the only growth area. In recent years there has been high demand for chefs, construction trades, hairdressers, health professionals and accountants amongst other professions.

Under the new recruitment drive, the government is actively seeking teachers, health and community workers, electricians, child minders, miners, construction workers, and other skilled trades as listed in the current Migration Occupations in Demand List (MODL).

Business services

This sector has grown considerably over the past ten years and is very diverse in employment opportunities. It embraces many of the services that are used heavily by corporate and government clients such as: legal, financial services, information technology, advertising and media.

As Europe is considered cosmopolitan and technologically advanced, professionals with skills in these areas will be highly valued by potential Australian employers, particularly in the larger cities including Sydney and Melbourne.

Health and education

If you are a nurse or doctor then you are in luck as Australia has been experiencing skills shortages within the nation's workforce in this area and is keen to attract overseas workers. Research shows that growth in health and education industries has been steady and is likely to increase in the future, especially in caring services due to factors such as an ageing population.

Nursing

Australia is desperately in need of nursing staff and most visa applications for nurses receive priority processing. Places of work vary as widely as Australia itself. Temporary and permanent visas exist to help nurses work in Australia's health care industry. Whether you can offer a high level of skills or need to gain additional skills, there will be a visa to suit you.

For further government/visa information:

www.immi.gov.au/migration/nurses.htm

Also refer to Healthstra, who are a provider of agency nurses to healthcare institutions in city and country areas. They can also help with visas, registration and getting work.

www.healthstra.com.au/travellers.htm

Lifestyle

'Lifestyle services' is a relatively new name that has been used to encompass a variety of industries including hospitality, recreation and entertainment. At the time of writing, these areas account for over 16% of job vacancies in Australia, compared with 11% in 1996. Some of this growth can be attributed to the 2000 Sydney Olympics but it is a trend that seems set to continue as Australian tourism continues to boom. This will almost certainly be boosted by the 2006 Commonwealth Games, which are taking place in the sports obsessed city of Melbourne.

Australia's capital cities are home to many of the country's tourist attractions and are generally the cultural and entertainment hub of their States. There are many opportunities for employment at leading establishments including international hotels, restaurants, galleries, museums, theatres, casinos, entertainment centres and retail outlets which offer a wide variety of positions from temporary work to senior management vacancies.

Industries in decline

It is also worth noting that some areas of industry have suffered significantly in the past few years and show few signs of recovering in the immediate future including: agriculture, forestry and some financial services.

UNEMPLOYMENT

In February 2006, the unemployment rate was 5.2% which is marginally higher than in February 2005 (5.1%) (source: Australian Labour Market Update April 2006). The unemployment rate was highest in the Northern Territory at 7.1% and lowest in the Australian Capital Territory at 3.3%.

PROSPECTS

Analysis shows that migrants with the best prospects for finding employment in Australia are professionals with high skill levels, college and university qualifications and strong proficiency in the English language. People in highly skilled occupational groups are also less likely to experience unemployment, which is a crucial factor when immigration is considering your visa application. For example, according to the Australian Labour Market Update Feb 2006, the unemployment rate for those who were formerly employed in their original country as labourers or related workers, was four times greater than that of professionals.

12
Researching the Australian Job Market from the UK

SOURCING INFORMATION

The following sites provide an invaluable insight into the current labour market and provide comprehensive and up to date information, which will undoubtedly help all prospective Australian job seekers. It would be advisable to take time in searching these sites for information relevant to you, well ahead of making your decision to relocate. You may save yourself enormous amounts of time and will equip yourself with the facts so that you can make an informed decision about your future plans.

Government based information

www.workplace.gov.au

This site contains a wealth of information for job seekers. Australian WorkPlace will help you find information on employment, workplace relations, government assistance, jobs, careers, training and wages. It also contains information which will give you the most update and comprehensive information about labour markets across the entire country. This may help you determine what sort of visa application you lodge as you should be able to determine whether and where in Australia there is a need for people with your particular skills.

There is a must-read publication on this site that will provide you with an in-depth overview of the current Australian jobs market.

Select the **Labour Market Information** section of the website, and click through onto Labour Market Information – **Skill Shortages & Vacancy Trends**. Within this section there will be a document named *Jobs Outlook*. This is a yearly publication which provides an overview of the skills projected to be in demand in the future and highlights occupations with good prospects.

Australian Jobs Update

Australian Jobs Update is a quarterly publication produced by the Department of Employment and Workplace Relations to aid the understanding of the labour market: www.workplace.gov.au under the information for migrants.

> **Brit tip**
>
> Whilst other documents on this site are designed for residents, the Jobs Update is specifically for overseas workers and migrants seeking work in Australia.

National state and skills shortage lists

This is a list of professions that are in short supply across Australia and the States. It will advise if the shortages are across the State or within regional or metropolitan areas.

Brit tip

These lists can be used to highlight areas of opportunity for British
workers across the States. This may be useful if you are planning on
applying for Skilled Independent Regional Migration or if you are
intending to reside in a particular metropolitan city.

Future Job Prospects

This site also predicts the prospects for a wide range of occupations up
to year 2010/2011.

Skilled Occupation List (SOL)

In order to migrate to Australia via Independent Skilled Migration, which
is the route explored by most professionals under 45, your occupation
must be on the Australian Immigrations Skilled Occupations List. This
falls into four categories:

- managers and administrators

- professionals

- associate professionals

- trade occupations.

All of the above lists can be found at:
www.immi.gov.au/allforms/pdf/1121i.pdf under 'migration', in
particular 'general skilled migration'.

Migration Occupations in Demand List (MODL)

When applying to enter Australia via the Skilled Independent visa
category you can earn extra points if your occupation is also currently on

the Migration Occupations in Demand List (MODL), which is current at the time that their application is assessed (not when their application is lodged).

The MODL list is *not* to be confused with the Skilled Occupations List (SOL), which is a visa prerequisite.

The MODL is reviewed annually to take into consideration existing and emerging skill shortages. Applications from persons who nominate an occupation on the MODL are **priority processed**.

In April 2005 the Australian government announced significant changes to its immigration strategy – adding 20,000 places to the skill stream of the country's 2005-2006 Migration Programme. As a direct result of this, it made additions to its Migration Occupations in Demand List (MODL). These changes are designed to help Australia meet its short- and long-term labour force needs.

The new skills on the MODL list include bricklayers, carpenters and joiners, cooks, dentists, plumbers, podiatrists and many more. All of these occupations, plus those already on the MODL, receive an extra 15 points and priority processing through Australia's points-style immigration programme.

An extra ten points will also now be allocated for State/Region sponsorship under the Skilled Independent Regional (SIR) visa to address the demands for more skilled migrants by many States and Regions.

'The changes reflect the government's strongly held view regarding the benefits of well managed immigration arrangements. A primary aim will be to increase the number of skilled migrants entering under the employer sponsored categories, as it is employers who are best placed to identify the skilled migrants we need,' said the Minister for the Department of Immigration and Multicultural and Indigenous Affairs (DIMIA), Senator Amanda Vanstone.

For the up to date and current MODL refer to:
www.immi.gov.au/migration

Additional information

www.myfuture.edu.au

Myfuture is an Australian career website that seeks to help people make career decisions, plan career pathways and manage work transitions. It contains information on trends of work and current vacancies, and provides tips on job applications, resumés and interviews.

PRIOR TO DEPARTURE FROM THE UK

The internet is a wonderful tool for research and it will allow you to check out the size of your chosen industry in the State you wish to reside in and identify the main companies. You may even be able to send your CV via email from the UK to relevant companies, which may provide you with some valuable feedback as to how buoyant the market is for people in your profession. At the very least it will provide you with a list of companies you can target when you arrive and their websites might supply you with their phone number or even list positions that are vacant. You will then be able to ring your targeted companies. The human resources department is usually a good place to start your fact finding mission.

INTERNATIONAL RECRUITMENT AGENCIES

A few of the UK's largest recruitment agencies offer help and advice on working in Australia. Some of them even list current vacancies and secure interviews for your arrival.

- www.michaelpage.co.uk
  This site enables you to search for current positions in Australia, particularly in finance, legal and sales and marketing.

- www.internationalcareers.hudson.com
  This website allows you to search for vacant positions in Australia and also provides information on what to expect in terms of work culture and lifestyle.

- www.robertwalters.com
  Robert Walters are specialists in finance, HR, marketing and legal recruitment. They have offices globally including the UK and Australia. You can view all international vacancies from this site and you can also request to speak to an international careers advisor who may be able to give you some valuable information on current positions available in your industry.

WORKING HOLIDAYS

Useful sites for Working Holiday visa holders

Some recruitment agencies specialise in helping Working Holiday Visa holders find temporary employment.

- www.worldwideworkers.com
  They specialise in quickly placing Working Visa holders in jobs from one day to three months.

- www.tntmagazine.com/au

  This is an invaluable site for people coming to Australia on a Working Holiday visa. Contains a wealth of information and links.

If you are on a gap year

- www.visitoz.org

  Visitoz helps young people with a sense of adventure and a Working Holiday visa (or other visas allowing work) to have employment on the land or in rural hospitality.

13
Starting Your Job Search

Hopefully by now you should have established that your occupation is in demand in Australia and that you can enter the country via one of the visa types. If you are like most people and do not have work already lined up there are many ways that you can enhance your job search, even ahead of your arrival.

Chances are that you will arrive with a clear idea of what kind of job you are seeking and which kind of companies might be in a position to offer you employment. There are some particularly useful websites for job seekers and I would recommend the following.

ONLINE TOOLS

• www.seek.com.au

• www.careerone.com.au

Both of these comprehensive sites allow you to search for current vacancies within all major cities and surrounds. They enable you to search by both location and industry, ensuring that you find the most relevant positions for your requirements. Depending on the job, you can either send your CV direct from the advert on the site or it will direct you to the relevant recruitment consultancy. The sites are updated daily and provide a great insight into the current market.

• www.ozjobsguide.com.au

This site provides an overview of the leading recruitment sites listing permanent, temporary and part-time jobs and allows you to click through. This is a particularly useful site for those wishing to cast the net wide.

* www.jobsearch.gov.au

This is a government run website that helps prospective job seekers. Not only does it contain up to date information about job vacancies in all the regions, it also offers useful tips and advice.

RECRUITMENT AGENCIES

As you would expect, all Australian capital cities have numerous recruitment agencies. The majority are based in or around the Central Business District (CBD). Many of them specialise in certain industries and it's a case of finding ones relevant to your profession which you can do by searching on line.

Brit tip

There's no hard and fast rule about how many agencies you can sign up with. All I would say is that Australian cities are small compared with the likes of Manchester, London etc so be careful that you don't flood the market with your CV. *Yellow Pages* is a good place to look for a list of recruitment agencies to contact, as is using the internet as a research tool.

PUBLICATIONS

As Australia is so vast and the cities are great distances from one another, there are no national newspapers. Each of Australia's capital cities has its own range of newspapers, which have useful information for job seekers. Refer to the city chapters to find relevant details.

CENTRELINK

Centrelink is a government job seekers initiative which has offices in many city suburbs and major country centres. It is a useful resource to know about as they can also refer foreign clients for overseas skills recognition and offer useful advice and information.

All job seekers can also use the free Job Network Access self-help facilities in Centrelink offices, which include telephones, photocopiers, fax machines, computers and daily newspapers.

You can locate them using the *White Pages* telephone directory or on their website.

www.centrelink.gov.au

YOUR RESUMÉ

Even if your CV is up to date and factually correct, it may need adapting for the Australian market.

Qualifications

Whilst most Australians are familiar with the UK and may have in fact worked there themselves, the chances are they won't be familiar with our universities and courses so make it clear what your qualifications are in and what they might be equivalent to over here. Your professional skills and qualifications may also need to be formally recognised by the appropriate Australian authority before you are allowed to work in some jobs.

Work experience

No amount of qualifications can make up for practical experience and skills and Australian employers will recognise this. Make it clear what experience you can offer as they may not recognise the name of the company you worked for or the position you held, so ensure your CV is straightforward and relevant.

Brit tip

Make your CV as Aussie friendly as possible. What I mean by this is don't make things too British focused – you need to make it clear that your skills, experience and qualifications are transferable.

JOB INTERVIEWS

Once you have secured an interview ensure that you have as much information about the company as possible. Investigate their product lines, their history and if possible their work culture as this can help you adopt the right attitude in the interview and will enable you to answer questions and ask any that you might have. Ensure that you dress in a manner befitting your industry.

SALARY EXPECTATIONS

The cost of living is a crucial thing to consider when moving to Australia as you must remember that wages are proportionately lower than in the UK. Salaries will vary across the States, with Sydney and Melbourne generally offering higher wages than other Australian cities, but this is comparative with the cost of living in those areas. You also have to remember that taxes in Australia are high. But the chances are that you aren't relocating to Australia to earn more money, so as long as you bear this is mind it shouldn't come too much as a nasty surprise.

Researching the market from the UK can also give you an idea of salary expectations, but don't fixate on this too much as there's a huge amount of difference between earning pounds and dollars. It is not until your pounds have run out that you truly understand the cost of living and that the Aussie dollars do not go as far as you think and certainly not as far as the British pounds!

Brit tip

When discussing salary, ask for the salary figure exclusive of superannuation as when included this can inaccurately inflate your pay packet by 9%. (See Chapter 5 for further information.)

WORKING CONDITIONS

Conditions in the workplace are generally very good in Australia. Annual leave within the majority of respectable companies is 20 days on top of the usual bank holidays. You have to love a country where they celebrate our Queen's birthday with a national day off work!

Australia is also a multicultural society and proud of this, therefore you should not expect to be discriminated against for your sexual preference or race.

Brit tip

• It is essential when job-hunting that you are contactable, as potential employers and recruitment agencies will soon lose interest in you if they can't track you down easily. You can pick up a pay-as-you-go mobile very cheaply, and internet cafés are easily accessible in the city and suburbs so you can log on to research companies and use email.

• Don't leave the UK without proof of your qualifications in the form of originals or at the very least good copies. Employers may well ask for them at the job offer stage and you do not want to delay starting work by waiting for papers to arrive from the UK, which could take weeks.

Part 3
VISAS AND IMMIGRATION

Adelaide

14
An Overview

Australian people are famous for their friendly and easygoing outlook on life. But anyone planning to come to Australia should understand that the Australian government is serious about protecting the security of their borders and are extremely strict about the visa application process. Australia's target migration intake is set yearly with a balance of different areas in mind, namely:

• skills

• family

• refugee/humanitarian.

Of these areas, there is a strong policy emphasis on boosting skills and business skills intakes. It is crucial that you apply for the correct visa type as you will only be considered in this category, even it if it is not the right one for you. It can be a time consuming and expensive process, therefore you must research this area stringently ahead of your application. I should also point that not everyone is eligible for an Australian visa.

THE CATEGORIES

There are three main categories of visas:

• migration

• temporary residence

• visitors.

I am assuming that if you are reading this book you intend to live and work in Australia, therefore only temporary and permanent residence will be discussed.

In general, visa applications need to be made outside of Australia and secured before your entry to the country. When applying, you must be 100% sure about the visa class you wish to be considered under as immigration will only process your application under this class – even if they know that you are better suited to another visa type. So do your research carefully.

15
Temporary Residence

This term is applied to anyone who is seeking to reside and work in the country on a temporary basis, with the intention of leaving again at the end of the designated period.

There are several visas in this type but in general the majority of British workers in this category apply from the UK under one visa type.

THE INTERNATIONAL RELATIONS STREAM

Working Holiday Visas (WHV) are designed for young people who are from countries with which Australia has working holiday arrangements, and who want to holiday and travel in Australia, while having the opportunity to work for short periods of time. Australia has reciprocal working holiday arrangements with the United Kingdom and Ireland amongst many other European countries.

Since 1997 over 258,000 Working Holiday Visas have been granted to British nationals (source Australian Immigration 2004).

A GUIDE TO THE WORKING HOLIDAY VISA

Providing you are aged between 18–30 and have no dependent children, travelling to Australia to holiday and working for up to a year should be fairly straightforward. However, you still need to secure the visa and you must adhere to some tight restrictions about what type of work you can do and for how long. You have to apply for this visa from the UK and it is essential that you have this visa in place before you make your arrangements to travel to Australia.

From the UK you should apply online by logging on to the immigration website: www.immi.gov.au/allforms/visiting_whm.htm

You will need to use the FORM 1150, paying the application fee with a credit card. You should expect to hear back from the Department of Immigration and Multicultural and Indigenous Affairs (DIMIA) within a relatively short period of time. If you are granted a visa online you will not have a visa label placed in your passport before entering Australia. This being the case, you will need to visit the nearest DIMIA office on your arrival in the country to have a visa label placed in your passport which will provide evidence of your right to work. Employers will ask to see this prior to hiring you.

This visa requires you to hold either a return ticket to the UK or proof that you have the financial means to go back to the UK or on to another country after your stay. It is valid for 12 months from the day you enter Australia and is a multiple entry visa, which will allow you to depart from and enter Australia as many times as you like during the year. However, there is no top-up of time available in Australia, if you choose to depart during the 12-month validity.

What restrictions are placed upon holders of this visa?

This visa will allow you to work for an employer for a period of up to three consecutive months. You must advise any potential employer of your working visa status. Should your working period extend over three months you will be in breach of your visa and could have it revoked if immigration catch you out. The visa is intended to supplement holiday travel – it is not intended for people to work the entire 12 months.

You can change from this visa to a Long Stay Temporary Business Visa if you can find a position that offers you sponsorship which will allow you to work for a company for up to four years. See section below on sponsorship.

Brit tip

- Working Holiday Visas are only granted once, so if you think there's any chance that you will just travel around the country instead of working then opt for an ordinary visitor visa. Don't waste this once in a lifetime opportunity on a whim.

- Should you return to the UK at the end of your 12-month visa and have worked during this time and paid tax, it may be worth lodging a tax return at the end of the financial year. This may entitle you to some money back. Also, you may be able to access any superannuation that you paid once you return to the UK. (For more information see Chapter 5.)

Recent changes to the Working Holiday Maker programme (WHM)

From November 2005 Working Holiday Maker visa holders will be able to apply for another WHM visa if they have completed at least three months' seasonal harvest work in regional Australia. Prior to this they were only able to secure one of these visa types in a lifetime. Australian immigration have brought in this change to encourage more young people to undertake seasonal harvest work, as many farmers said that these visa holders are amongst their most valuable workers because of their enthusiasm and mobility.

This change will mean even more Working Holiday Makers will become available to Australian farmers. It will also benefit other industries, as

WHMs who do harvest work and stay on in Australia for another year will be available to work in industries such as tourism. To assist the smaller states and regions access more skilled migrants, WHMs and Occupational Trainee visa holders will also be allowed to apply for and obtain a Skilled Independent Regional visa while still onshore. This then provides a pathway to permanent residence.

Over recent years the WHM programme has grown significantly from less than 50,000 per annum in the mid-1990s to approximately over 100,000 in 2004-05. This is expected to grow further in 2005-06.

SPONSORSHIP

Temporary employer-sponsored workers

If you have chosen not to apply for permanent migration then the chances are that you will arrive on a Working Holiday Visa as many under 30s do. This will restrict you to working for a maximum of three months within a particular company. Most backpackers and travellers don't seek work for any longer for this three month period so it's not an issue for them. However, there are lots of Brits who arrive in Sydney, immediately fall in love with the place and then seek a position that will enable them to live and work in Sydney longer than their one year Working Holiday Visa will allow them to.

This can be achieved by seeking a position with a company that can offer you sponsorship. This allows you to exchange your working visa for a Long Stay Temporary Business Visa which entitles you to live and work in Australia for up to four years.

Frequently asked questions on sponsorship

How do I go about getting sponsored?

How easily you can secure sponsorship is completely dependent on what kind of industry you are in and what skills you can offer. On the whole larger, more established companies are in a better position than smaller ones to offer potential employees sponsorship. This is for a variety of reasons:

- It costs companies several thousands of dollars in admin fees to secure a business visa for their employee – smaller/family run companies don't usually want to meet these costs.

- Most larger companies use immigration specialists (such as Price Waterhouse Coopers) to help with their employees' visa issues – this is particularly useful as they have the experience and knowledge to help secure your business visa.

- The larger the organisation, the more opportunities there may be for skilled British professionals.

Do I need to have certain skills and experience in order to achieve sponsorship?

As with all of the other working visa types, your employer will need to prove that your skills are needed by them and that they cannot find anyone within the current Australian labour force to meet their requirements. This then allows them to sponsor personnel from overseas on a temporary basis to work in Australia for up to four years. Sponsored individuals can come from a wide range of professions including sales, marketing, business management, finance, IT, publishing, law etc. They are judged on a case by case basis and are dependent on current local market shortfalls in skilled professionals. You should apply for positions in the usual ways (via recruitment agencies, job ads, on spec etc) and then ascertain the sponsorship opportunities at interview stage.

Are there any recruitment companies which can help me achieve sponsorship?

There are third party companies which can help you with your job search for a sponsored position. Providing you meet certain criteria in terms of qualifications and experience they may be able to help you secure a position using their expertise and contacts in the jobs market. They can offer you useful advice and will lodge your paperwork, thus increasing your chances of a successful application enormously. They can also help you achieve the maximum tax benefits that you may be entitled to under the terms of this visa. Of course these companies aren't offering their services for free so it is worth noting that they will take a certain percentage in fees and charges. You may well decide that this is worth it, especially if it secures you (and your partner) a four-year visa.

Brit tip

- To maximise your potential in securing a sponsored position as quickly as possible, contact a company such as Freespirit to search on your behalf whilst simultaneously job-hunting via your own methods.

- If your potential employer is not in a position to sponsor but does offer you a great job then don't panic – you might still be able to take it and secure a visa by other means. You should contact one of the umbrella companies. Even if they have not found the job for you they can still apply for a sponsorship visa on your behalf.

- Companies do not advertise the fact that they offer sponsorship. During your interview they are likely to ask you about your visa status. At this point you should say that you would be looking for sponsorship and assess their reaction. If they are a large international company the chances are that they will have at least one overseas employee who may well be sponsored by them.

'Freespirit', through its clients, have many vacancies to fill which require the services of highly skilled individuals. They have become a leader in the application for Business Sponsorship (457) visas for overseas professionals wanting to live and work in Australia. In particular, they seek to place professionals from the following industries: IT, telecommunications, banking and finance, sales and marketing, accounting, management, recruitment and engineering.

www.freespirit.com.au

What happens after I am offered a position with sponsorship?

There is a fair amount of paperwork involved which your company's HR dept, or immigration agent (or umbrella company) can help you with. You will need to submit your CV, which may need tweaking, and you may need proof of your qualifications. You will also be required to undergo a medical and a chest examination. You can start working for your company on your working holiday visa as long as it is still valid or on a Bridging visa if it has run out. Your visa should come through as long as there are no hiccups within two to eight weeks, depending on Immigration's work load.

> **Brit tip**
>
> Strike up a good relationship with your HR dept, immigration agent/umbrella company and make sure your paperwork is in order and information is to hand. They know precisely what immigration is looking for in order to ensure your application is watertight so make them your new best friends!

What implications does sponsorship have for my spouse or partner?

If you are married or in a *de facto* relationship only one of you needs to secure sponsorship in order for you both to change to long stay visas. This will allow your spouse or partner to work without restrictions for whomever they choose for the period of the visa.

Are there any costs to me?

Not usually, if your company has decided to sponsor you they generally pick up all of your visa application costs.

Restrictions for employer-sponsored workers

As a condition of your visa, you are not allowed to change employer or occupation without prior authority from Immigration or without having a new sponsorship deal in place. If you are in discussions with any company you must ensure that they are in a position to sponsor you, otherwise you will lose your work rights within Australia.

Benefits for employer-sponsored workers

Sponsorship brings with it some rather wonderful tax allowances. As you have proved that you are employed in a position that an Australian was not able to take at that point you can claim certain living away from home allowances, also known as LAFHAs. As the term 'allowance' suggests, it can provide significant tax benefits for the average employee. Precisely which LAFHAs you are entitled to receive will depend on your employer.

Brit tip

- You should raise the issue of LAFHAs at your contract stage with the HR department. It is wise that they are written into your contract, and they can't be backdated, so you should seek to reap their financial benefits as soon as possible.

- If you have a partner or dependant on your sponsorship visa you may be able to claim LAFHAs for them as well, so do ask.

Applying for permanent residency

You can apply for permanent residency in Australia during your sponsorship. This is easier to achieve when already living and working here than by applying from the UK. You will still be liable for all the visa related costs, and the process may be lengthy, but there are many migration experts who can help you maximise your application chances.

16
Permanent Residence

Permanent residence refers to all people wishing to reside in Australia permanently and make it their primary country of residence.

The migration programme for 2004-05 had 120,000 places available for migrants, with a strong focus on attracting skilled people and people who agree to live in regional areas of Australia. The government determines the level of the migration programme on an annual basis.

THE MIGRATION PROGRAMME

This is made up of:

1 A **Skill Migration stream**, which has a number of categories for people who have particular occupation skills that are in demand in the Australian labour market, or outstanding talents or business skills.

2 A **Family Migration stream**, where people can be sponsored by a relative who is an Australian citizen or permanent resident.

3 A **Special Eligibility stream**, which includes former Australian residents who have maintained ties with Australia.

SKILL MIGRATION STREAM

Employer sponsored migration

The permanent employer sponsored migration schemes offer three options for Australian employers to nominate skilled overseas staff to take up positions that cannot be filled from within the Australian labour market or through the employer's own training programmes.

The **Employer Nomination Scheme** enables Australian employers to nominate highly skilled staff whose occupations are listed on an official list. Positions on the list are generally those requiring a three-year post secondary school qualification (ie a degree). The positions are to be full-time, available for a period of at least three years and offer a salary at least matching that shown on the list for the occupation.

Applicants are to be highly skilled and able to demonstrate their skill level in any one of three ways:

- by having their qualifications assessed by the relevant assessing body plus having three years of relevant post-qualification work experience

- has been nominated to fill a highly-paid, senior executive position

- or by having spent two years working in Australia on a 457 (or other stipulated temporary) visa, the last 12 months of which are to have been with the sponsoring employer.

The **Regional Sponsored Migration Scheme** (RSMS) enables regionally based employers to nominate overseas workers to fill positions located in regional Australia that cannot be filled from within the Australian labour market. Regional Australia is all of Australia except Brisbane, the Gold Coast, Sydney, Melbourne and Perth. Under the RSMS scheme, the sponsoring employer approaches an appointed regional body to obtain certification that the vacancy is genuine. An RSMS visa applicant is required to have a two-year diploma or higher qualification that is relevant to the appointment.

Applicants under the RSMS should normally be less than 45 years of age and have functional English language skills. As with the ENS, there are provisions within RSMS for exceptional circumstances to be taken into account. Where a position is so unusual or highly specialised that the employer is unlikely to find anyone who meets the established criteria to fill the vacancy, exceptions to the age and English language requirements can be made. This will depend on the circumstances that the employer outlines to demonstrate the special skills required and difficulties experienced filling the position.

Labour Agreements are formal arrangements that enable Australian employers to recruit a specified number of workers from overseas in response to identified or emerging labour market or skill shortages. The skill level required for entry under a Labour Agreement is determined on an individual agreement basis and takes into account the specific needs of individual employers. Applicants are expected to have qualifications and experience that are suitable for the agreed position, and how that is determined can differ across occupations and industries.

There are other ways for people to enter the country, including via the Humanitarian Progamme which is in place mainly to help people in desperate need to leave their own country for safety reasons (ie refugees). However, most British workers enter Australia via the **Migration Programme** and in particular via the **Skilled Migration stream**.

Skilled migrants for permanent residence

The skill stream of Australia's migration programme targets people who are highly skilled, are under 45 years of age, and who will quickly make a contribution to the Australian economy. There are a number of categories in the Skill stream to enable successful business people and highly skilled and qualified personnel to migrate to Australia. These include:

View from Opera House, Sydney, NSW

Kanagaroo on the road out of Mungo National Park, NSW

Sunset, Broken Hill, NSW

Bunda Cliffs, Great Australian Bight, SA

Broken Hill Sculpture Symposium, The Living Desert Reserve, Broken Hill, NSW – *Under the Jaguar Sun*

Russell Falls, Mt. Field National Park, TAS

Bottlenose Dolphin, Monkey Mia, WA

Hawksbill Turtle, Great Barrier Reef, QLD

Black Tip Reef Shark, Great Barrier Reef, QLD

Koala, Healesville Sanctuary, outskirts of Melbourne, VIC

Blowholes, Gasgoyne area (70km north of Carnarvon), WA

Uluru, Uluru-Kata Tjuta National Park, NT

Twelve Apostles, Port Campbell National Park, VIC

Eyre Highway, Nullarbor Plain, SA

Wineglass Bay, Freycinet National Park, TAS

Tamarama Beach, Sydney, NSW

- **Skilled Independent**: for people selected on the basis of their skills, age and English language ability.

- **Regional/Skilled Migration**:   enables Australian state and territory governments and regional employers to nominate skilled migrants for entry on the basis of development objectives and identified skill needs. State/territory governments that choose to participate in the scheme conduct an audit to establish what skills are in short supply and in what locations.

- **Skilled – Australian sponsored**: people selected on the basis of their skills, age, English language ability and family relationship. In each case they must be sponsored by a relative already living in Australia. Special conditions apply for people whose sponsor lives in the Sydney metropolitan area or a 'selected area' in New South Wales as defined by postcode. See: www.immi.gov.au

There is another visa type available within the skilled migrant section (called **Skilled-Designated Area Sponsored**); however, this visa is not available to people migrating to large cities, so will not be discussed in any more detail.

www.immi.gov.au

Most British people seeking to migrate to Australia fall into the Skilled Independent visa type.

This category is for people who are under 45 years of age, and have skills, qualifications and employability that will contribute to the Australian economy.

Requirements for the Skilled Independent visa

1   Satisfy the basic requirements (under 45, fluent in English, have a degree, diploma or trade qualifications and have working

experience) in any skilled occupation that is on the SOL (see below). The work experience can be waived if, within six months of applying, you complete an Australian degree, diploma or trade qualification at an Australian educational institution after a minimum of two years' full-time study.

2 Nominate a skilled occupation from the Skilled Occupations List (SOL). When you apply, you must nominate an occupation which fits your skills and qualifications and it must be on the SOL – FORM 1121i on the immigration website. The list is far too comprehensive to include in this book and covers an enormous range of occupations. Points are awarded for each occupation ranging between 40–60 points. To ensure your occupation is on there refer to the Skilled Occupations List (SOL) on the immigration website.

3 Your skills must have been assessed as suitable for working in your nominated occupation by the relevant assessing authority. The name and contact details are provided in Form 1121i. You will need to have obtained your skills assessment before you apply for your visa.

4 Pass the points test.

The points test

This test aims to ensure that the applicant has the skills necessary to allow them to quickly enter the Australian workforce.

At the time of going to print points are awarded for:

• Skill (range between 40–60 points depending on your nominated occupation – refer to form 1121i).

• Age (the younger you are the more points you will be awarded – between 15 and 30 points available).

- English language ability (competent English 20 points/vocational English 15 points).

- Specific work experience (between 5 or 10 points available).

- Occupation in demand. A number of occupations/specialisations have been identified as being in demand in Australia. They are listed on the Migration Occupations in Demand List (MODL) on the immigration website. (Applicants can be awarded extra points under this factor or if they have a job.)

- Australian qualifications. Applicants with Australian qualifications may have a greater chance of employment in Australia. (Extra points are available to applicants who hold Australian qualifications – 5, 10 or 15 points available. Applicants who can claim points for Australian qualifications may also be eligible to claim 5 points if they lived and studied for at least two years in regional Australia.)

- Spouse skills. An extra 5 points may be awarded if your spouse also satisfies the basic requirements of age, English language ability, qualifications, nominated occupation and recent work experience and has obtained a suitable skills assessment from the relevant assessing authority for their nominated occupation.

- Relationship (for Skilled–Australian sponsored only). Points for relationship may be awarded if an applicant or their spouse has a relative who is an Australian citizen, a permanent resident or an eligible New Zealand citizen, and who is willing to sponsor them.

Bonus points can be awarded for one only of the following: capital investment in Australia; Australian skilled work experience; or fluency in one of Australia's major community languages, other than English.

To check current points test requirements and for further information refer to www.immi.gov.au and search for 'points test'.

Brit tip

- When making a joint visa application, only one person is assessed so couples should choose the partner with the best prospects of scoring sufficient points to reach the pass mark.

- You must score sufficient points to reach the pass mark. If your score is below the pass mark but equal to or above the pool mark, your application will be held in reserve (in the pool) for up to two years after assessment.

Category	Current pass mark	Current pool mark
Skilled-Independent (offshore)	120	70
Skilled-Independent Regional (provisional)	110	110
Skilled-Australian sponsored	110	105
Skilled-Independent (onshore)	120	120

Skilled Independent Regional Visa (SIR)

This visa type is only available for those who are willing to live and work outside of metropolitan areas, who meet the regional skills shortages in that particular region and are sponsored by a state or territory authority. The SIR visa is points-tested and provides an option for people if they either do not meet other skilled migration visa requirements or choose to live and work in rural areas. All areas of Australia are covered except Sydney, Newcastle, Wollongong, NSW Central Coast, Melbourne, Perth, Canberra, Brisbane and the Gold Coast. The SIR visa supports State and Territory governments seeking to sponsor skilled migrants who commit to living and working in regional Australia. Successful applicants are granted a three-year temporary visa with the prospect of permanent residence at the end of that period.

Recent changes affecting skilled visa applicants

In April 2005, the Australian Government announced significant changes to its immigration strategy by adding 20,000 places to the Skill Stream of the country's 2005–2006 Migration Programme and additions to its Migration Occupations in Demand List (MODL). The changes will help Australia meet its short- and long-term labour force needs. Refer to www.immi.gov.au and search for 'MODL'.

The new skills on the MODL list include bricklayers, carpenters and joiners, cooks, dentists, plumbers, podiatrists and many more. All of these occupations, plus those already on the MODL, receive an extra 15 points and priority processing through Australia's points-based immigration programme.

An extra 10 points will also now be allocated for State/Region sponsorship under the Skilled Independent Regional (SIR) visa to address the demands for more skilled migrants by many States and Regions.

Conditions as stated by DIMIA

SIR applicants must be less than 45 years of age at the time of application (unless their skilled visa application was placed in the pool and they have been invited to apply for a SIR visa), have vocational English language ability, post-secondary qualifications (or equivalent work experience), have an occupation on the Skilled Occupation List (SOL) and recent work experience in a skilled occupation, or have recently completed an Australian qualification.

After two years of living and working/studying in a low population growth metropolitan area, the visa holder will be eligible to apply for permanent residence and reside elsewhere in Australia.

Business Skills

The Business Skills visa class of Australia's migration programme encourages successful business people to settle permanently in Australia and develop new or existing businesses. Under the two-stage arrangements introduced in 2003, business migrants are granted a Business Skills (Provisional) visa for four years and, after establishing the requisite level of business or maintaining their eligible investment, are eligible to make an application for a Business Skills (Residence) visa.

FAMILY MIGRATION STREAM

You can also apply to migrate through Partner Migration if you are the spouse of an Australian citizen or permanent resident. The spouse category covers both marriage and *de facto* relationships with their sponsor. If you are applying as a *de facto* you have to have been in the relationship for at least a year prior to your visa application. Fiancé(e)s can also apply under the Prospective Marriage Category but must be outside Australia to do so and engaged to their sponsor with plans to marry. An additional visa is available for those in Interdependent Relationships which includes same-sex couples. Those who can apply under the interdependent partner category must be at least 18 years old and in an interdependent relationship with their sponsor. Parents and children of Australian residents and permanent citizens also have the opportunity to apply for a visa via the Family Migration stream.

Brit tip

When applying for your visa you must be very sure of which visa class you wish to be considered under as immigration will only consider your application under this section – even if this may not be the most appropriate visa type for you. Check the immigration web site for classifications and ensure that you have done your research to make your application as watertight as possible.

THE APPLICATION PROCESS

Health checks and character references

All applicants and their families applying for permanent residency will be required to undertake a medical examination and a chest examination X-ray if aged 11 years and over. You will also be required to take an HIV test if aged 15 years and over. Australian immigration rules require that all visa applicants wishing to stay in the country more than 12 months must meet a character requirement. This will involve a check which may require you having to obtain a certificate of no criminal record from a police station. You should check your status at the time of application.

Visa costs

There will be costs in obtaining your visa. These will vary enormously depending on what type of visa you are seeking and how complicated your case is, but it is worth noting that they can potentially run into thousands of dollars (Australian).

All costs must be paid when you apply for your visa or travel authority.

Please note that whatever the outcome of your application, this charge is non-refundable.

Application times

Visa processing times will vary depending on many factors. It is worth noting that the application process can be lengthy, according to the category applied for, but categories such as regional migration are accorded priority processing. Your migration advisor or immigration office will be able to provide you with an estimate of how long your particular application will take.

IMPLICATIONS OF RETURNING TO THE UK

Generally, the longer a permanent resident remains outside Australia the more difficult it is to return there as a permanent resident.

New migrants are issued with a multiple re-entry visa when their immigration application is approved. These visas allow holders to travel to and from Australia as permanent residents for up to five years from the date of being granted. Once that initial visa has expired the holder must obtain a Resident Return Visa (RRV) if they wish to continue to travel outside Australia and return as a permanent resident.

The purpose of RRVs is to facilitate the re-entry into Australia of permanent residents and to ensure that only those people who have a genuine commitment to residing in Australia, or who are contributing to Australia's wellbeing, retain the right to return and remain permanently.

To be granted an RRV, an applicant must meet certain crucial criteria, as listed on the immigration website – check for further details. An RRV cannot be extended. It is generally not possible for a permanent resident who has resided overseas for over five years to be granted an RRV unless they can demonstrate that they have substantial ties to Australia and compelling reasons for their absence.

Part 4
CITY-BY-CITY GUIDE

Sydney

17
Living in Sydney and NSW

State: New South Wales (NSW) – 'The First State'
Size: 801,428 sq kms (10.5% of Australia's total area)
Capital: Sydney
Population: 4 million (NSW total pop. 6.7 million)
Time zone: + 10 GMT
Telephone area code: + 61 2

THE STATE

New South Wales is a beautiful and diverse State, offering something for everyone. Aside from the delights of its capital Sydney, NSW comprises endless beaches, stunning mountain ranges, World Heritage National Parks and quirky towns.

Regional NSW

Regional NSW has much to offer new migrants. Many consider the lifestyle advantages of a relaxed quality of life and close-knit, friendly communities ahead of the bustle and expense of living in the State's capital.

The growing popularity of large inland centres like Dubbo and Tamworth, and coastal cities such as Newcastle, Wollongong and Coffs Harbour, has turned what were once quiet and sleepy villages into cosmopolitan regions with fabulous sporting, entertainment and leisure activities. Food, drink, music and wine festivals are held regularly in country NSW and have attracted an international following. Aside from the obvious lifestyle advantages, your hard earned money stretches considerably further once outside the expensive Sydney suburbs.

British skilled workers may also find their willingness to live and work outside of metropolitan Sydney enhances their chances of securing an appropriate Australian work visa.

The city

Stylish, sexy and sophisticated, Sydney is the gem of the southern hemisphere. It is Australia's prized possession. It is the capital of New South Wales and Australia's largest city with a population of over four million people. Sydney is also one of the most popular destinations globally for international visitors. The city is built around one of the most beautiful harbours in the world which is home to the world famous landmark, the stunning Opera House. The majority of Sydney's whopping 37 beaches are situated within 30 minutes of the city centre with kilometres of golden beaches stretching north and south of the city on the shores of the Pacific Ocean. Even the Prime Minister chooses to live in Sydney rather than in his official residence in the country's political capital Canberra, so it's no surprise that many Brits take one visit here and never go back to the UK!

SYDNEY'S HISTORY

Europeans first charted the east coast in 1770, when the well-known Pacific explorer, Captain James Cook, reached Australia. The First Fleet, comprising 11 ships and around 1,350 people, arrived at Botany Bay where they discovered upon anchoring that there was no fresh water available locally, therefore they headed further north to Port Jackson which is now known as Sydney Harbour.

The British first used Sydney as a penal colony with over 750 convicts arriving on the first ships into port. At the time of their arrival, the Sydney area was home to the Eora, one of several hundred Aborginal groups living in Australia. However, the British did not take kindly to sharing their new land and over many years forced them out of their land or in worse cases killed them.

In 1901 the six British colonies in Australia formed a federation to become the Commonwealth of Australia. This marks the period of the modern country. Sydney continued to grow and by 1925 became a metropolis of one million people. This grew to two million by 1963 and in the years since the area has continued to prosper and grow into the stunning city it now is, well deserving of its worldwide reputation.

THE CLIMATE

Sydney's climate is one of its most attractive features. Summer in Sydney is from December to February; autumn is from March to May; winter is from June to August, and spring is from September to November. The summer months have an average maximum temperature of 28°C. Being close to the ocean, the hot days are cooled in the evening by refreshing sea breezes and evening temperatures are balmy – perfect for relaxed outdoor dining which is a way of life in Sydney. June to August are the coolest months, with daytime temperatures rarely falling below 7° Celsius. Compared with Britain, the weather is simply stunning all year round.

THE PEOPLE

Sydney is a wonderfully friendly and fun city to live and play in.

The beaches and harbour play a major role in the lives of Sydneysiders and swimming, running, sailing, surfing, and generally being outdoors as much as possible play a huge role in people's daily lives. With such beautiful weather and scenery on hand you can understand why. Much of the city is surrounded by areas of protected natural bushland and there are parks and gardens at every turn. As many Australians are practically brought up in the surf, any spare moments see the young and old flock to the beaches to 'sunbake', swim and surf or just hang out with friends – not to mention any excuse to have a barbie which is a tradition that I promise you will come to love!

Gay and lesbian Sydney

Sydney is a dream come true for gay and lesbian migrants and visitors. It has a buzzing and ever-increasing gay and lesbian community, strong anti-discrimination laws and, of course, the annual Sydney Gay and Lesbian Mardi Gras which is an event shared by the whole community and truly not to be missed!

Oxford Street in Darlinghust is the heart of the gay scene in Sydney. By day, the many cafés are filled with locals enjoying a coffee and a gossip, but by night the action hots up and the bars and clubs are always busy with boys and girls enjoying the delights on offer.

On the other side of town, in Sydney's inner-west, lie the suburbs of Leichardt and Newtown, which are also popular with the gay community.

- www.ssonet.com.au *Sydney Star Observer* is Australia's highest circulation gay and lesbian newspaper with a circulation of over 31,000 copies per week. It focuses on news, entertainment and information for the gay and lesbian community. Travel features are published fortnightly.

- www.gaytravelguides.info *Gay Travel Guides* is Australia's leading gay and lesbian travel publisher.

THE ATTRACTIONS

Most of Sydney's incredible tourist attractions are conveniently located either within, or in close proximity to, the central business district, or at points around the harbour.

Opera House

Sydney's most famous landmark is, of course, the spectacular Opera House, which is truly breathtaking and the venue for many great occasions. The Opera House has become Sydney's cultural centre, offering opera, ballet, concerts, drama, and film and the Botanical gardens that surround it are a great place to picnic or walk at weekends.

The Bridge

Sydney Harbour Bridge is an incredible structure and an Australian icon even by today's standards. Built in 1932, the bridge is an engineering masterpiece and still dominates the harbour's stunning skyline. It has also become a lucrative tourist attraction as bridge climbs are offered daily.

The Rocks

The harbour foreshore is home to the historic Rocks area, the site of Australia's first European settlement in 1788, and now home to a variety of galleries, museums, restaurants and shops. It houses the largest concentration of historic buildings in Sydney with a story to tell of the city's colourful past. A good way to familiarise yourself with the area is to take The Rocks Self-Guided Walking Tour which takes in the most significant historical sites and explains the enclave's colourful and dark past.

Royal Botanic Gardens

Occupying the headland between the Domain and the Opera House, the Royal Botanic Gardens make for wonderful relaxing walks and provide some of the city's finest green space. The location is second to none, offering stunning views of the harbour and surrounds. It also makes for a good, safe place to sit and relax under one of the 200 year-old trees and enjoy a picnic whilst watching the outdoor theatre in the summer months. Within the grounds, there is a formal rose garden, succulent garden, oriental garden, herb garden and fernery. It is also home to an abundance of wildlife including many different species of birds and bats.

Bondi Beach

There are few more alluring sights in Sydney than the golden sands and crystal clear waters of Australia's most famous beach, not to mention all of the beautiful people who frequent it on a daily basis. Bondi is home to one of the oldest surf life saving clubs in the country and is a mecca for locals and tourists who flock there to sunbake and surf. It has a thriving entertainment scene with many bars, cafés and restaurants all taking advantage of the stunning ocean views and famous sunsets. The beach walk between Bondi and Bronte beach is one of the most popular in Sydney, offering incredible coastal views at every turn.

GETTING AROUND

You have a wide range of options for moving around the city. On the whole, public transport is clean, reliable and generally offers a wonderfully efficient service in New South Wales. You might hear Sydneysiders comment otherwise but they can't have been to England as in comparison it is a pleasant experience! Of course it helps that for most of the year any waiting time is spent catching rays as opposed to trying to shield yourself from the wind and rain as in Blighty.

Buses

Sydney Buses operates an extensive network of bus services throughout the city. The main bus terminals are located at Circular Quay, Town Hall and Central Station. They are a cheap and reliable way of getting around the city and local suburbs.

Brit tip

Purchase a 'travel tens' bus pass. These can be purchased from most newsagents and transport agents and allow you ten bus trips. They do not have an expiry date and save you 30% on each trip. They are ideal if you make either frequent or occasional travel and ensure you are never fumbling for change. www.sydneybuses.nsw.gov.au

Trains

Metropolitan services

CityRail has a large range of leisure and tourist tickets to get you where you want to go. Martin Place station is located in the heart of the CBD district and allows you to take trains around the city and its suburbs. It also offers an efficient route to the airport. Ticket vending machines are open 24 hours.

Interstate and intrastate services

Central Railway Station is the main junction for interstate and intrastate rail services.

Brit tip

For information about routes and timetables for trains and buses call the Sydney Transport Infoline: 131 500.

Ferries

One of the most delightful ways to make your way to and from the city is to take a ferry on Sydney Harbour. Many city workers commute daily from the northern beaches and surrounds via the many ferry services which are reasonably priced and efficient.

> **Brit tip**
>
> For information about routes and timetables for the ferries call Sydney Transport Infoline on 131500 or online at www.sydneyferries.info

Light rail

Metro Light Rail is Sydney's newest transport system but its routes are fairly limited at present, therefore it is generally only used by people commuting between the areas it currently services: Central Station, Chinatown, Darling Harbour, Star City Casino, Sydney Fish Markets and Wentworth Park. It does, however, run 24 hours a day, seven days a week.

> **Brit tip**
>
> For more information call the Infoline 02 9285 5600 or online at www.metrolightrail.com.au

Monorail

The monorail takes you on a loop round the city. It only has eight stops through the CBD and is used by tourists rather than every day Sydneysiders, as it's a fun way to see the city and the views are good.

Taxis

Taxis are generally yellow and can be found in abundance. You can either book one over the phone (Taxis Combined – 02 8332 8888) or simply hail one from the street. They are reasonably priced.

Airport

Sydney's Kingsford Smith Airport is located in Mascot about 10 km and a 30-minute drive southwest of the central business district and Sydney Harbour. It is a busy airport that has an international and domestic terminal.

CARS AND DRIVING

Once you have arrived in Sydney you may well be in need of transport, especially when house hunting etc. Renting a car is a convenient solution to getting around Sydney in the short term and allows you to get your bearings. In Australia they drive on the same side of the road as in the UK (ie the left) and in general the roads are excellent and traffic does not cause the same problems as it does in UK cities. Do make sure that you pick up a local map or street finder which you will find invaluable in getting around.

Car rental

In Sydney the majority of the large car rental companies are located at the airport and also just outside of the city in the area known as Kings Cross. You will recognise all of the big names as they are global brands including Hertz, Avis, Thrifty, Delta, Budget and Europcar. Most of the cars on offer are automatics; however, manuals are available on request. You will need your British driving licence and a credit card as many companies require a deposit.

> **Brit tip**
>
> In my experience, I have found that by far the cheapest car rental rates are on offer from a local company called Bayswater based in William Street, Kings Cross, Sydney. As you would expect, discount rates are achieved the longer you rent for and this company makes renting a car extremely reasonable.

Useful contacts

- Bayswater car rental Sydney 02 9360 3622

- Budget car rentals Sydney 13 2727

- Avis car rentals Sydney 13 6333

- Hertz car rentals Sydney 1300 132 607

- www.vroomvroomvroom.com.au allows you to compare prices of all large car rental companies across Australia and highlights specials and promotions.

> **Brit tip**
>
> For directions and maps of Sydney refer to www.whereis.com.au

Taxis

Taxis are a reliable and well-priced way to get about and can easily be hailed from the street or pre-booked.

- Taxi Combined Services 8332 8888

- Silver Service Taxis 13 3100.

Obtaining a NSW licence

If you hold a British or International Driver's licence you can hire cars or drive on Australian roads.

If you are entering the country with a permanent visa or intend to reside in NSW for longer than three months then you are no longer considered a visitor and will need to obtain a NSW licence. Please refer to the following website for further information:

www.rta.nsw.gov.au

18
Renting a Home in Sydney's Suburbs

AN OVERVIEW

Since the 2000 Sydney Olympics the property market has boomed in NSW and there is an enormous range of highly desirable homes within the city and surrounding areas. There has been a noticeable increase in development, and both homeowners and property developers have been very savvy in recognising the profitability of the rental market. This led to the market being flooded with high quality refurbished houses and apartments. However, there is a constant demand for decent rental properties of which there are many to be found. Of course these costs do vary enormously from suburb to suburb. As the cost of living is greater in Sydney than in any other city it should be noted that rental prices also reflect this.

Costs

Properties located in and around Sydney typically cost far more than those in country areas around the State. Houses in Sydney's top waterside suburbs, such as Mosman and Vaucluse, often fetch up to ten times more than their counterparts in the outer suburbs.

Finding your home

I am presuming that unless you are staying with family or are a lottery winner that you will be looking to rent a home. As you can imagine there is an enormous variety of properties available in the Sydney rental market. As in any other city, costs vary depending on location, size and condition.

Good places to start

*   McGrath: Rental hotline 1300 888 389
    www.mcgrath.com.au

Renowned Australian property agent McGrath's website is comprehensive and provides current property listings across all of Sydney and surrounds, including contact number and viewing times. This site is particularly useful as it contains a wealth of information about each suburb, which may be useful to you if you have not visited the country before.

*   LJ Hooker: General enquiries 1800 621 21
    www.ljhooker.com.au

Another detailed site that provides comprehensive and up to date information on current rental properties that might be of interest.

Brit tip

*   Each of the regions in Sydney and surrounds are serviced by local free weekly magazines which contain the most up to date list of rental properties and times/dates they are viewing that week. You can find the publication that's relevant to your area by popping into a local newsagent and asking them for the latest edition as most stock them.

*   For more detailed information please refer to Chapter 8.

Shopping for your Sydney home

If you are moving in and around the Sydney and Eastern Suburbs areas it is worth visiting the Supacentre at Moore Park. This is a huge retail site – a short car or bus ride from Sydney city out towards the airport – that has many of the big-name home furnishing retailers and electrical stores. Most of the shops will deliver at an additional cost if your home falls within their catchment area.

For location details and store opening hours etc refer to: www.supacenta.com

2ndsWorld

It is well worth taking a trip to 2ndsWorld. As the name suggests, this store stocks factory seconds electricals including carton damaged, factory run out models as well as brand new gas and electrical appliances – all directly from the manufacturers complete with the manufacturers' warranty. It is well established and a trip to one of their four Sydney stores can lead to massive savings on all your home appliances. There are four 2ndsWorld stores in metropolitan Sydney – for further details and store locations refer to: www.secondsworld.com

THE INNER WEST

The Inner West comprises many interesting suburbs that are close to the city and are easily accessible by bus and car, making them desirable areas to live.

Popular suburbs include: Balmain, Glebe, Newtown and Liechardt.

> **Brit tip**
>
> For rental accommodation in this area check out the *Inner Western Suburbs Courier*, the weekly free magazine for this area which lists available properties and viewing times:
> www.innerwesterncourier.com.au

THE EASTERN SUBURBS

Many of Sydney's most fashionable places to live are located in the Eastern Suburbs. They can all be accessed from two main roads which lead directly out of Sydney's CBD, making them very desirable due to their proximity to the city and surrounding beaches.

Popular residential areas include: Darlinghurst, Paddington, Woollahra, Surry Hills, Bondi Junction, Double Bay, Point Piper, Rose Bay and Vaucluse.

> **Brit tip**
>
> For rental accommodation in this area check out the *Wentworth Courier*, the weekly free magazine for this area which lists available properties and viewing times:
>
> www.wentworthcourier.com.au

SOUTHERN BEACHES

Bondi Beach

The iconic image of the bronzed lifesavers has appeared on travel shows around the world and secured Bondi's position as the beach to be seen at. However, it is not the most beautiful of Sydney's beaches.

Bondi's close proximity to the city makes it a popular place to live, especially with the Brits who long to live by the sea but wish to access the CBD easily (it's about a 25 minute bus ride into town).

Bondi has an eclectic mix of people residing there – the surf attracts many travellers and young people who mix happily with the urban professionals and the elderly who spent their lives by the beach. Many types of people enjoy the vibe that Bondi offers. There is a long parade running along the front of the beach which offers an enormous range of bars and restaurants catering to all tastes and budgets. On top of this are internet cafés, surf shops, backpackers' hostels and hotels.

Other beaches

Heading south from Bondi, the beaches are: Tamarama, Bronte, Clovelly, Coogee, Maroubra and Cronulla.

Brit tip

For rental accommodation in this area check out the *Southern Courier*, the weekly free magazine for this area which lists available properties and viewing times: www.southerncourier.com.au

---

NORTH SYDNEY

North Sydney is a satellite commercial centre just across the Sydney Harbour Bridge from Sydney city. It has few visitor attractions as it is an office centre for a wide range of major companies in computers, communications, insurance, travel and so on. It is also the gateway to the Lower North Shore, which follows the headlands and inlets of Sydney Harbour towards Manly. The North Shore is an affluent residential area with large houses offering some of the best views across the water to the city.

North Sydney is surrounded by some of the prettiest harbour side suburbs: Kirribilli, Milsons Point and McMahon's Point, each of which has a village atmosphere and is fun to visit. All three have beautiful views across the harbour to the city.

Brit tip

For rental accommodation in this area check out the *Sydney Weekly Courier*, the weekly free magazine for this area which lists available properties and viewing times: www.sydneyweekly.com.au

---

NORTHERN BEACHES

Manly is known as the entertainment centre for the Northern Beaches. Surrounded by water on three sides, it is popular with all sea lovers offering fantastic surf, swimming and sailing. It offers residents a good range of well priced property, particularly apartments, and is popular with Brits who enjoy all it has to offer including a quick ferry ride into the city.

Heading further afield, the Northern Beaches continue onwards from the city and include Dee Why, Collaroy, Newport and the stunning Palm Beach which is more commonly known as the Home and Away beach as this popular television series was filmed there.

Obviously there are many other regions and excellent residential areas; however, there will be commuting timings and cost implications.

TO FIND OUT MORE

For an idea of property rental costs in any of these regions refer to the following sites:

- www.realestate.com.au

- www.domain.com.au This site will allow you to look at current rental properties across Sydney and its suburbs and will provide you with an accurate idea of what each area gives you for your dollars. You can also click on to detailed suburb guides, which will tell you all you need to know about the area, including schools.

Chapter 19
Recreational Sydney

You will never be short of things to do in Sydney and NSW. Thankfully, as the weather can be relied on most of the time, Sydneysiders spend most of their time outdoors. The beach plays an important role in people's lives here as most of them have grown up with one foot in the surf!

IN THE WATER

None of Sydney's beaches is ever empty and from sunrise to sunset you will find joggers, sun worshippers, tourists and dog walkers enjoying the bountiful sand that Sydney has to offer. Where there's water there are surfers, who can always be found in abundance, come rain or shine. The surfers' preferred beaches are Bondi and Manly – which also offers good diving for all scuba enthusiasts. There are plenty of reserves as well which offer safe, calm swimming and are a pleasant alternative to the beach for non-sand lovers.

ON THE WATER

If sailing is your passion or if you have always wanted to learn to sail then you have come to the right town! One of the first things you'll notice when in the harbour and surrounds are just how many yachts and boats are on the water at any one time. As well as being the ultimate status trophy, boats are a way of life in Sydney and Australia in general. Cruising in a sailboat on a beautiful sunny day, taking in the incredible sights of the world famous Opera House and Harbour Bridge, truly is a magical and memorable experience that I can't recommend highly enough. Should you be interested in sailing lessons then check out the listings in local papers and magazines or search the internet for classes. There are many companies in the Quay and harbours that offer cruises including sunset and dinner trips. Similarly there are opportunities to fish in and around the harbour, although you should be aware that there are restrictions and rules to be adhered to. If you prefer to see your fish alive and well then the place to visit is the Sydney Aquarium. It is one of the world's most impressive aquariums with more than 5,000 different Australian fish displayed in their natural habitats. Visitors can 'walk on the ocean floor' through 145 metres of acrylic underwater tunnels, including the infamous shark tank which is home to some of the world's deadliest sharks. New attractions include a new seal sanctuary where both little and big kids can pass the hours watching the seals at play through the underwater walkway.

OUT AND ABOUT

Parks are plentiful in Sydney, even in the city, and can be found at every turn offering a pleasant alfresco dining experience for office workers who escape their office confines to read the paper and have a sandwich with friends.

The largest of the parks is Centennial, in between Paddington and Bondi Junction, which is a popular venue for cyclists, walkers, rollerbladers, picnickers and horse riders. There is a large equestrian centre nearby which is open to the public for rides or lessons. In the summer months, this park hosts the Moonlit Cinema where they screen new and classic movies under the stars. People flock to the park after work to meet friends, armed with blankets and picnics, to enjoy their favourite flicks and have a glass of wine whilst the local bats fly overhead. Not a bad way to spend the evening. There is also an outdoor cinema during the summer at Lady MacQuaries Chair which is next to the botanical gardens close to the Opera House. This venue is nothing short of stunning as the screen literally comes up out of the water and the view across the city and harbour bridge on a warm evening makes the evening worthwhile, even if the movie isn't up to scratch!

CULTURAL SYDNEY

Sydney certainly knows how to entertain its millions of visitors and there's no shortage of things to do come rain or shine in this vibrant city. It is a mecca for arts and culture lovers and there is something for everyone throughout the year including a wealth of festivals celebrating jazz, film, opera, theatre, ballet, food and drink amongst others.

Summer festival

In the summer the outdoor activities and festival season kicks in, offering a fantastic and diverse range of things to do including a range of events in the Domain which is a large park in the city. It hosts a series of free jazz, opera and classic events that are well worth attending. The Botanical Gardens also host other outdoor events in the summer including children's and adults' theatrical performances. Aside from these, there is a wide range of ticketed festivals throughout Sydney ranging from food and wine shows to pop festivals, arts and crafts events to the crazy and wild Mardi Gras – Sydney really does offer something for everyone.

Sydney Opera House

One of the world's greatest contemporary buildings, the Opera House was completed in 1973. Its various theatres host concerts, ballet, opera, drama and dance performances. Even if you don't want to take in a show, it's worth a visit just to marvel at the breathtaking workmanship that was involved in making this globally renowned masterpiece.

Art Gallery of NSW

Some of Australia's finest artists have their work on show here. The Aboriginal material is an exciting part of an interesting collection that includes Asian and European art. The local works of art offer a disparate view of Australian society and culture and there is always a programme of special exhibitions.

Sydney Theatre Company

Founded in 1978, the STC operates out of its home venue, The Wharf, on Sydney's harbour, and at the Drama Theatre and the Playhouse of the Sydney Opera House. The annual season features both local drama and theatrical classics.

SPORT

Sydney's affiliation with sport was made spectacularly obvious when they hosted the hugely successful 2000 Olympic Games. The many impressive sports stadiums and facilities are still put to good use as the city continually plays host to a wealth of international events. Sydneysiders turn out regularly to support their teams although they are not such fanatics as their Melbourne rivals. They are also just as likely to be found playing sports as watching them.

Telstra Stadium (Homebush) is one of the country's largest stadiums with an 80,000 + capacity. The centrepiece of the Sydney 2000 Olympic Games, Homebush is a regular host to international sports and music events. The Sydney Cricket Ground (SCG) is the major ground in Sydney for cricket and the nearby Aussie Stadium (formally known as the Sydney Football Stadium) is also used for soccer, rugby league and union.

Rugby

Sydney is one of the world capitals of rugby league. The main competition, run by the National Rugby League, is the Telstra Premiership, which includes interstate sides. The other big rugby league series is the State of Origin, played in Sydney and Brisbane. The NSW versus Queensland game generates a lot of passion. Many international games are also played locally.

AFL

Australian Rules football is a unique, exciting sport run by the Australian Football League (AFL). The Sydney Swans are Sydney's team who play home games at the Sydney Cricket Ground (SCG).

Soccer

Soccer is gaining in popularity, thanks in part to the success of the national team and to the high profile of some Aussies playing overseas. The national league is only semi-professional, and games attract a relatively small following, but there is a huge amateur league, which includes more than its fair share of Brits!

Brit tip

- If you are interested in playing for a local team, of which there are many, the following site can help you source one in your area. It can be a great way to meet people. www.soccernsw.com.au/home

- Footie season runs from February to September.

Golf

NSW has more golf courses than any other Australian State and Sydney has some of the best, which are located around the city's centre.

FOOD AND DRINK

Sydneysiders enjoy nothing better than dining out with friends and family, ensuring that the many cafés and restaurants are always busy. The city's thriving eateries are well spread throughout the city and inner suburbs, catering for all tastes and budgets, and locals and tourists really do take advantage of what's on offer. Alfresco dining is popular and with views such as the Opera House and Bondi Beach, you can understand why.

Over recent years, Sydney restaurants have attained a reputation for producing fine cuisine based on the freshest of ingredients. Besides world-renowned Modern Australian cuisine, expect to try fine cuisines from Asia, including Thailand, Vietnam, and China, as well as familiar European dishes.

Most Sydney restaurants offer an extensive selection of red and white wines, so you will have every opportunity to accompany your meal with a fine Australian wine. Many Sydney restaurants allow you to bring your own wine – look for the BYO (bring your own) symbol or ask when you make a booking.

Most Sydney restaurants are reasonably priced and you can expect to pay from $9–$20 for entrées and from $15–$35 for main meals. Lunchtime prices are always less expensive than dinner rates.

For a guide to Sydney restaurants: www.sydneyrestaurants.com

SHOPPING

As you would expect, Sydney shopping is a pleasurable experience. The city has many malls with globally recognised shops and brands including the exclusive fashion houses of Gucci, Versace and Louis Vuitton amongst others.

The two largest well known malls in Sydney city are Pitt Street Mall, which is an outdoor pedestrianised shopping area with many high street retailers including David Jones and Meyer, and the beautiful and historical Queen Victoria Building which offers boutique shopping at its best.

There are plenty of retail opportunities outside of the city. Paddington is well known for its funky shops which run all the way down the very aptly named Oxford Street. Check out the quirky weekend markets including Bondi, Balmain, Glebe and Paddington for one-offs.

Bondi Junction also recently became home to the stylish Westfield Centre that has every shop under the sun, not to mention bars, cafés and a cinema.

Factory outlets

One of the largest factory outlet centres can be found a short drive from Sydney city at Birkenhead Point. This centre is home to over 120 fashion, homeware and food stores including Bayswiss, Freedom, David Jones Warehouse, French Connection, Insport and Nine West amongst many others. As with most factory outlets, each time you visit your experience will vary depending on what's on offer at that point but as all the shops are under one roof it is well worth a visit as there are bargains to be had. You can also reach the outlet centre by hopping on a direct ferry from Circular Quay or the number 500 bus.

www.birkenheadsc.com.au

NEW SOUTH WALES ATTRACTIONS

Sydney may be the capital of New South Wales but this huge State has many more treasures in its vast chest to experience, many of which are only a few hours away.

Blue Mountains

To the west of the city lies the spectacular World Heritage listed mountain range, home to many famous Australian attractions including the world's steepest railway ride and the Three Sisters – a stunning rock formation that has become a NSW icon. It is a popular destination for Sydneysiders, who take advantage of the cooler climates to enjoy weekend retreats or simply make the short journey to hike through the lush forests.

The Hunter Valley

www.winecountry.com.au

Less than a two hour drive from Sydney's CBD lies the most visited wine region in Australia – the Hunter Valley. It is home to Australia's oldest and one of its greatest wine areas, though it produces only a tiny proportion of its wines. Its proximity to the city ensures that it is a popular weekend destination for tourists and Sydneysiders, who are keen to enjoy the fresh air and sample all of the delights of this stunning area. It is host to many food and drinks festivals throughout the year and many international artists hold outdoor concerts in the vineyards during summer months.

The Central coast and the Hawkesbury

The Central coast stretches about 200km from Sydney to Newcastle. This beautiful area is filled with National Parks and beach resorts. In less than two hours' drive from Sydney CBD you can find yourself in the peaceful surroundings of the Hawkesbury River, which reaches from Brooklyn, to the historic towns of Windsor and Richmond. It is an unspoilt region of natural beauty, comprising National Parks, waterways and quaint villages. Many visitors hire houseboats, which offer a pleasurable and leisurely way to take in the sights.

USEFUL INFORMATION

For further information on NSW and Sydney:

www.visitnsw.com.au

Useful NSW Information:

- Sydney operates on Eastern Standard Time (EST), which is calculated by adding ten hours to Greenwich Mean Time (GMT).

- Daylight Saving begins in Sydney on the last Sunday in October and finishes on the first Sunday in March. During this period clocks are advanced one hour and time is then calculated by adding 11 hours to GMT.

20
Working in Sydney

Quality of life factors are important for attracting migrants to any country. Australia's high quality of life and western culture make it a very attractive place for expatriates. Sydney benefits further from its high profile image overseas which is well deserved as it offers an incredibly high standard of life for most people.

COST OF LIVING

It should come as no surprise that the cost of living is higher in Sydney than in any other city in Australia. As previously mentioned Sydney became the twentieth most expensive city in the world to live in as revealed by Mercer's annual study (2004). The city jumped a staggering 47 places in one year – a fact that cannot be ignored when thinking of moving to Sydney.

Wages are generally higher than other State capitals but, despite this, Sydney and NSW can sometimes feel costly to live in on a daily basis. Property prices went through the roof after the 2000 Olympics and kept on rising, making it virtually impossible for first time buyers to gain a foot on the ladder. Rental prices also remain on the high side; however, there are still some good deals to be found especially if you are prepared to live in an up and coming suburb.

Entertainment is also on the pricey side with dining out costing more in Sydney than anywhere else in Australia. However, travel and groceries are comparable with the likes of Melbourne and Brisbane.

Current economic overview

For detailed and up to date information about living and working in Sydney refer to: www.business.nsw.gov.au

For a current overview of precisely what opportunities there are in the local workforce for people with your skills log on to the following site. It will also give you an overview of which industries are currently on the increase/or decline:

www.myfuture.edu.au and click through to facts which will provide you with current labour market information.

EMPLOYMENT

Leading industries

New South Wales' economy is highly diversified, with strengths in a broad range of sectors.

Sydney is home to many of the world's leading financial institutions and blue chip companies including HSBC, Ernst & Young and AMP. It has a high percentage of skilled workers as it is a highly desirable city in which to work and the local economy is thriving. Finance, legal, media, IT, HR and marketing professionals are found here in plentiful numbers. Sydney is also the base for the majority of the country's leading radio and television services. The central business district is dominated by office-based corporate and public sector employment. At the same time, NSW boasts significant strengths in agricultural and minerals production, as well as in manufacturing and processing.

OPPORTUNITIES AND LIMITATIONS FOR SKILLED MIGRANTS

Sydney continues to attract foreign workers to its shores in large numbers; however, employment opportunities may be restricted to those meeting stringent visa requirements. This is due to the fact that Sydney and NSW in general is *not* short of skilled workers who can fill the local job vacancies, unlike many other rural regions. There therefore tend not to be as many vacancies and opportunities for migrants as in other parts of the country and it is unlikely that you would be able to migrate to Sydney under the Regional Skilled Migration visa which tries to tempt workers into areas of the country where they are desperate for skilled migrants.

HOW TO FIND OUT IF YOUR OCCUPATION IS IN DEMAND

If you are thinking of moving to Sydney under the Skilled Migration stream be sure to research the current local jobs market and ensure that your position is on the Australian immigrations Skilled Occupation List ahead of applying for a working visa: www.immi.gov.au and, using the search tool, enter 'skilled occupation list'.

Also refer to the Migration Occupation in Demand list in Sydney/NSW. Should the State currently have high demand for people with your experience your chances of securing the visa you need may be enhanced: www.immi.gov.au

If there is not a shortfall in skilled workers in your nominated occupation then immigration may not be able to grant you a visa. They will not risk you being unemployed or taking jobs away from Australians (remember they do have the legal right to prevent non-Australians or residents applying for any advertised post).

At the time of writing this book, occupations in demand in Sydney and NSW include engineers, medical/nursing staff, legal experts, teachers, marketing professionals and IT workers.

Recruitment agencies

Once you have established that there is work for you in Sydney or NSW you can start your job search. Recruitment agencies are located across the city and in larger suburbs. Some of the companies are international such as Reed, Robert Walters and Select; others are local. To find an agency to suit your needs refer to the jobs pages of local newspapers or use on-line resources as detailed in Chapter 13.

Temporary/casual work

Holders of Working Holiday visas should easily gain temp or casual work, especially in the summer months and holiday periods. The following sites are a good place to start your search and provide an idea of the type of work available.

• www.sydneybackpackers.com.au

Although this is aimed primarily at travelling workers, it provides a useful guide to casual/temporary work opportunities.

• www.indysbackpackers.com.au click on to 'work contacts'.

Aimed specifically at backpackers/working holiday makers, this site contains a useful list of Sydney based recruitment agencies.

Publications

The *Sydney Morning Herald* has a supplement specifically for job seekers on Wednesdays called RADAR. The weekend paper also has a comprehensive pull-out job section. If when walking round the city you get offered a copy of *9-5* or *CityWeekly* then do take it as these two weekly free publications also have job sections and are especially useful for banking/legal/financial and PA vacancies.

EDUCATION

According to the Australian Immigration website there are over 2,200 primary and secondary schools in the NSW government school system, located throughout NSW. Children usually attend their local school, although parents may apply to send them to schools which are not in their area. To find a school in NSW refer to: www.schools.nsw.edu.au/schoolfind/locator/index.php

In NSW children from age 6 to 15 must go to school. However, many children start earlier.

Primary school

Primary school attendance is compulsory for all primary school age children.

High/secondary school

Most students aim to complete the NSW Higher School Certificate to qualify for some technical courses provided by the Technical and Further Education (TAFE) colleges and for admission to universities.

Fees for non-residents

There are cost implications for non-residents (temporary resident visa holders) when sending children both to state schools and private schools. They start at approximately $4,500 per child, per year for state schools and are upwards of this figure for private.

For detailed information about costs and requirements, refer to the NSW information package for temporary visa holders: www.schools.nsw.edu.au and click on to the international students' section.

University of Sydney

This is one of the largest universities in Australia, offering the widest range of courses in the country and boasting the largest university library in the Southern Hemisphere: www.usyd.edu.au

Childcare

As you would expect from such a cosmopolitan city, there are many companies offering high standards of quality childcare throughout the region. To find out further details or to locate one in your area refer to: www.cityofsydney.nsw.gov.au and click on to 'community' then 'childcare'.

21
Living in Melbourne and Victoria

State: Victoria (VIC) – 'The Garden State'
Size: 227,600 sq kms
Capital: Melbourne
Population: 3,200,000 – second largest city
Time zone: + 9 GMT
Telephone area code: + 61 3

VICTORIA

Victoria covers an area of approximately 227,600 sq km, which represents 2.9% of the total land area of Australia and is about the size of England, Wales and Scotland combined. Victoria's population of around 4.8 million people makes up about 27% of the total Australian population, second only to NSW.

www.visitvictoria.com

MELBOURNE

Melbourne is Australia's second-largest city and the capital state of Victoria. It is a vibrant and exciting city offering a fantastic standard of living to its 3.6 million residents. It is a haven for lovers of art, music, sport and culture and has an action packed annual events calendar that puts other countries to shame. The city has always enjoyed a friendly rivalry with Sydney and although it lacks the iconic landmarks of its neighbour, Melbourne's pleasures stem from the enormous diversity of its people. The city also offers great shopping and fabulous bars and restaurants. Melbourne is also the sports capital of Australia and its residents are nothing less than fanatical about it. Fortunately for them the sporting calendar is jam packed with international events throughout the year, including the Grand Prix and the Australian Tennis Open. www.melbourneaustralia.com.au

THE HISTORY

Melbourne has been home to indigenous populations for 50,000 years. The first Europeans settled in 1834 and the founder is said to be John Bateman, who was so taken with the place he is said to have written the following in his diary: 'This will be the place for a village'. It was then purchased from the Doutgalla tribe for an annual tribute of trade goods worth about £200. The Federal government was established in Melbourne in 1901, where it remained until 1927 when Canberra took over as the seat of the national government. Named after Lord Melbourne, then British Prime Minister, the fledgling city prospered and grew as it has continued to do in the decades since.

THE CLIMATE

Melbourne is said to have 'four seasons in one day'. This is due to the fact that although there are distinctions between the four seasons, the weather on a day-to-day basis can be somewhat unpredictable. In general, summer days are sunny and warm and winter is cool. The other seasons are somewhere in between. It's always useful to carry extra layers so you can adjust your clothing accordingly.

THE PEOPLE AND CULTURE

Victoria's population is the most culturally diverse in Australia and this trend is set to continue as people continue to migrate there, attracted by all its wonders. A quarter of Melbourne's residents were born overseas and although English is still the primary language, there are some other 140 languages spoken. Over the years, the constant flow of settlers from Europe, the Middle East and Asia have helped to create the cosmopolitan metropolis that exists today. This wonderful mix of international cultures influences everything you see, do and eat in Melbourne. The city is very liberal and permissive and Melbournians are proud of the fact that different cultures, classes and sexualities coexist in relative harmony.

THE ATTRACTIONS

Sydney may have the world famous Opera House but Melbourne has more than a few treasures of its own. With renowned architecture, extensive parklands, café lined streets and international festivals, Melbourne's attractions are visible all year round.

Melbourne Cricket Ground (MCG)

The MCG is the Wembley Stadium of Australian sport and entertainment, and is the venue for huge sporting and music events. Although the MCG is arguably one of the most important cricket grounds in the world, it is much more than a cricket ground to the sports crazy people of Melbourne. It is one of the great icons of the city, worshipped by the locals, and is a reflection the enormous fascination Victorians have with sport.

Royal Botanic Gardens

Established in 1846 by the first Governor of Victoria, Melbourne's Royal Botanic Gardens are considered among the world's finest. They contain extensive landscaped gardens covering 86 acres and are home to more than 51,000 individual plants, representing over 12,000 different species. The gardens have become a natural sanctuary for native wild life including black swans, bell birds, cockatoos and kookaburras, filling the air with their distinctive song. In the summer months you can enjoy Shakespeare plays in these beautiful surroundings.

Federation Square

The size of an entire city block, Federation Square was the city's most ambitious development in recent years. Built in the very heart of the city, it was designed with the aim of being the city's cultural hub and has successfully become a place where people get together and share local events. It is the home of a wealth of attractions, including galleries, cinemas, restaurants, cafés, bars and host to many festivals and events. There is a large screen and stage that are put to good use all year round, and residents and visitors turn out in thousands for the free outdoor events.

Old Melbourne Gaol

Built in the mid 1800s, the Old Melbourne Gaol was a dominant symbol of authority and prior to its close in 1929 was the scene of 135 hangings including Australia's most infamous citizen, Ned Kelly. Open to the public, visitors can take tours through the jail's torture rooms and cells, which are filled with grisly reminders of the past including death masks and lashing instruments, and examine the scaffold on which Ned Kelly was hanged.

National Gallery of Victoria

Opened in 1861, this is Australia's oldest art gallery and frequently holds interesting exhibitions.

Queen Victoria Market

This popular open-air market is the largest in the Southern Hemisphere, and a hub for trade and commerce, as well as the many visitors who enjoy sampling its tasty delights.

Southbank

This is the buzzing riverside promenade stretching along the south side of the Yarra River from the popular Southgate shopping and dining complex to the glitzy Crown Casino. It's a favourite spot for Melbournians to drink, dine and stroll. Southbank is the area that stretches along the southern bank of the Yarra River. Southbank was once an old and neglected area, mostly industrial, which has recently been rejuvenated as the heartbeat of the central city area. The Victorian Arts Centre buildings and the National Gallery of Victoria are both on the south bank.

Brit tip

Pick up a copy of the very useful monthly free guide *Melbourne Events* which will give you the heads up on what's going on in town.

Outdoor leisure is high on the list of priorities for Melbournians, who take advantage of the temperate climate and the city's proximity to the sea. Going to the beach, hosting BBQs, wining and dining *al fresco* or sipping coffee at one of the numerous restaurants and cafés in and around Melbourne are favourite pastimes.

Parks and scenery

Melbourne is frequently referred to as being the world's most liveable city and this is due in part to its outstanding array of parks and gardens. It boasts more than 650 hectares of beautiful public gardens and parklands. South of the city near St Kilda Road, other major parks include the Fawkner Park, Flagstaff, and Fitzroy Gardens, Queen Victoria Gardens and Kings Domain. Another famous Melbourne greenland is Albert Park and Lake, home to the Australian Grand Prix, which attracts tourists from all over the world for this reason alone. Cyclists, roller bladers, joggers and golfers also take advantage of this beautiful park.

A GUIDE TO MELBOURNE'S SUBURBS

In recent years there has been a large population growth in the inner-city area, with many people choosing to live in the city's pleasant suburbs. Not only are they within close proximity of the city but they also offer residents the village vibe that is currently so desirable. Living in these areas allows Melbournians to enjoy all the culture and attractions of the city whilst simultaneously enjoying the beauty of the surrounding gardens, parklands and beaches.

Each area is distinctive and has its own charm, history and defining characteristics, ensuring there is a diverse mix of people residing in the inner north, south, east and west suburbs.

City of Melbourne

The city of Melbourne is the economic, political and cultural hub of Victoria. It contains the Port of Melbourne (the most significant port in Australia) and major advanced manufacturing facilities, as well as a concentration of universities and research institutions. The centre itself is laid out in a grid system and houses a combination of modern high-rise and beautiful historical buildings. Over the past five years an increasing number of residents have moved into the central business district and immediate surrounds, bringing renewed life to the region. The smaller city streets hide some of the best Greek, Italian and other cosmopolitan eateries.

St Kilda

Not to be confused with St Kilda Road, St Kilda is a buzzing suburb, south of the city, and is a playground for residents and visitors alike. It is one of Melbourne's most high profile and fashionable suburbs known for its cosmopolitan nature and unique charm. It has a wealth of trendy boutique and great eateries. St Kilda Beach is very lively, especially in summer, and is easily accessible by road and tram. This bayside suburb is just far enough away from the city centre to retain its unique charm and to have a vitality of its own.

South Yarra

This is one of the more exclusive areas of Melbourne and real estate here is very expensive. South Yarra and neighbouring Prahran are renowned for their great shopping. There are many great clothing shops to choose from, ranging from budget to the very expensive, and most of these are located on Chapel Street. The area also has great cafés, restaurants and an active nightlife.

East Melbourne and Richmond

East Melbourne is a pretty Victorian area where the residential houses are made up of rows of Victorian terraces.

Richmond is one of the city's earliest settlements, and is a vibrant suburb based around food and fashion. Best known for its bargain designer and seconds shopping along Bridge Road and Swan Street, Richmond is home to the factory outlets and seconds stores for many of Australia's finest fashion and accessory designers. Richmond is also known for being the heart of Melbourne's Vietnamese community.

Fitzroy

To the north of the city centre is Fitzroy. Traditionally a hub for Melbourne's artistic community, the area has become a fashionable residential district and is now home to inner-city urban dwellers, attracted to the bohemian lifestyle and village atmosphere. A short stroll along Brunswick Street will give you a feel for this popular suburb. It has many cafés, restaurants and funky secondhand shops. You will also notice the strong Latin/Spanish presence which is evident in the clubs, tapas bars and stores in the area.

Carlton

Carlton is the traditional home of Melbourne's Italian community and is famous for the bustling restaurants and cafés that spill on to busy Lygon Street.

Greek quarter

Astonishingly, Melbourne boasts the world's third largest Greek-speaking population. Should you visit the areas around Lonsdale and Russell Streets you could be fooled into thinking you are in Greece itself as they have been the meeting place for Melbourne's Greek community since the early 1900s. Every March hundreds of thousands of visitors gather to pay tribute to the greatness of Greece and celebrate the annual Antipodes Festival.

South Yarra and St Kilda Road

St Kilda Road is Melbourne's most beautiful and prestigious tree-lined boulevard. Along St Kilda Road you can experience everything from fine art, theatre and stylish dining to magnificent parks and historical monuments.

Flinders quarter

This is Melbourne's version of New York's Soho and is known locally as The Quarter. Once home to Melbourne's rag trade, Flinders Lane now houses funky designer boutiques, fashion warehouses and Australia's largest concentration of commercial art galleries. Artists, musicians and writers live harmoniously side-by-side.

Chinatown

Chinatown is a distinctive area of Melbourne that dates back to the goldrush days of the 1850s. Incredibly, Chinatown is the oldest continuous Chinese settlement in the western world.

RENTING A HOME IN MELBOURNE

Melbourne is the second most expensive city in Australia to live in and house prices reflect this fact. The 2006 Commonwealth Games are also set to push prices even higher as the area feels the benefits of increased tourism boosting Melbourne's economy.

Having said that, there is still likely to be a wealth of good quality, affordable homes and of course as in any location, there is housing to cater for all tastes and all budgets.

Choosing where to live

Things to consider in Melbourne:

- Do you want to live near to a beach?

- Do you want an apartment or a house?

- Commuting times.

- Budget.

- Other factors such as proximity to schools, childcare accessibility, etc.

Finding your home

There are a variety of options you can choose from when it comes to sourcing rental properties:

- *The Age* newspaper under the Domain section on Wednesdays and Saturdays advertises apartments and houses available through real estate agents or private listings.

- Suburban newspapers also advertise rental properties.

- Rental listings are available from real estate agents.

Online

You can also search for property online at the following sites, which will also give you a good idea of rental prices across the suburbs.

www.liveinvictoria.vic.gov.au

www.realestateview.com.au/rent_res_vic.html

GETTING AROUND

Melbourne's public transport system is unique. It offers three modes of transport – trains, trams and buses – with Melbourne being the only city in Australia to operate an extensive tram system as part of its public transport network.

Brit tip

Melbourne's automated ticketing system operates on all train, tram and bus services in the metropolitan area with electronically encoded tickets called Metcards. These provide you with flexible travel on any of the three modes of transport and can be pre-purchased from many places around Melbourne.

Trams

Melbourne's green and yellow trams are a familiar sight and are an efficient and easy way to get around the city. All of Melbourne's suburbs are linked by trams, which are a convenient form of transport.

Brit tip

The burgundy coloured City Circle Tram is a free service that runs every ten minutes in a loop past Melbourne's well-known attractions. This is a good way to see the city and get your bearings.

Rail services

There are two main railway stations in the CBD:

- Flinders Street Station is the main terminus for Melbourne metropolitan rail services.

- Spencer Street Station is the main hub for country rail services.

Buses

A wide-ranging bus network travelling all over the city and its suburbs complements Melbourne's trains and trams.

> **Brit tip**
>
> NightRider Buses offer safe, affordable transport from the city to numerous suburban destinations on Saturday and Sunday mornings, departing hourly between 12.30am and 4.30am. NightRider buses leave from the corner of Swanston and Collins Streets.

For train, tram and bus information call Metlink on 131 638 or visit www.metlinkmelbourne.com.au

Taxis

The Victorian taxi industry has more than 4,000 distinctive yellow taxis delivering service 24 hours, seven days a week.

- Black Cabs: 13 2227
- Silver Top Taxi Service: 131 008

Car rental

- Budget: 13 27 27

CHILDCARE

There are currently 25 childcare centres in the City of Melbourne, four of which are owned and managed by the City of Melbourne. Fees are approximately $50 per child per day with reduced rates per week.

For details of childcare facilities across Victoria: www.cccav.org.au

22
Recreational Melbourne

Melbourne has a reputation as Australia's most events orientated state and rarely a week goes past without the city celebrating art, music, film or sport. Melbournians are spoilt for choice by the sheer wealth of entertainment and events available throughout the year in their vibrant city.

CULTURAL MELBOURNE

After one visit to Melbourne, you cannot fail to appreciate why it is internationally renowned as the arts and cultural capital of Australia. Lovers of opera, art, music, dance and comedy will be in awe of the dazzling array of entertainment on offer all year, in and around the city. Diverse culture can be found at every turn from the city lanes to regional centres such as Heidelberg and Elwood. The area of Southbank is a cultural hub and home to the Victorian Arts Centre, the National Gallery of Victoria, the Australian Ballet, Melbourne Symphony, the Victorian College of the Arts and Playbox Theatre Company.

Each year the Melbourne Fringe Festival spices up the city's cultural calendar with an entertaining programme of groundbreaking and daring performances ranging across all art forms.

Theatre

Theatre lovers are spoilt for choice as every night of the week curtains rise on stages across the city, to reveal the latest Broadway sensation or a new take on an old classic. In the summer months, visit the Royal Botanic Gardens for outdoor performances of Shakespeare.

Comedy

The Melbourne International Comedy Festival attracts a wealth of talent from around the world and, for several weeks in March, laughter can be heard throughout the city. Throughout the rest of the year the numerous venues host comedy evenings ranging from established stand-up comedy acts to open mic nights.

www.comedyfestival.com.au

Galleries

The city's many galleries are packed with quality works reinforcing Melbourne's reputation as a leading influence on Australian art. Melbourne is also home to the National Gallery of Victoria (NGV), Australia's oldest public gallery and home to one of the country's most important art collections.

For 17 days each October, the Melbourne International Arts Festival features unique international and Australian attractions in the fields of dance, theatre, music, opera, visual arts and includes free and outdoor events.

www.melbournefestival.com.au

Music

Whatever your taste in music, you can find it in Melbourne. The city's pub culture sees many local acts playing at smaller venues whilst international artists regularly play the big entertainment centres. Annual music events include the International Music Festival to Melbourne in February and the Umbria Jazz Festival.

Museums

Melbourne's museums document the city's history and offer exhibitions as diverse as the city itself, from Aboriginal pieces to the sets of cult TV show *Neighbours*! The recently built Melbourne Museum, with its distinctive roofline and grand proportions, is the largest museum not only in Australia but also in the whole Southern Hemisphere.

GAY AND LESBIAN

No one can argue that Melbourne isn't gay and lesbian friendly. Melbournians are proud of their liberal views to sexuality and seize the opportunity to tell the world as often as possible! Key events in the calendar include:

- The Midsumma Festival which takes place over three weeks in summer, and is a gay and lesbian celebration of events including a pride march, carnival day and picnic.

- The Melbourne Queer Film Festival which is held every March, and shows local and international features, documentaries and short films during this ten-day festival.

Brit tip

To find out what's on locally, pick up one of the free gay and lesbian newspapers which can be found at local newsagents – titles to look out for include *Bnews*, *Melbourne Star* and the *Melbourne Community Voice*.

SPORT

Melbourne is a city with a worldwide reputation for its fanatical following of sport and the city is proud of its history of staging successful international sporting events. It is the home of many of the world's largest tournaments and the Melbournians turn out in their thousands to enjoy them. Sydneysiders do not share the same enthusiasm for following and participating in sports as their southern counterparts. Historians claim that Melbournians' huge fascination with sport eminated from the city's resentment at coming second to arch rival Sydney with regards to climate and spectacular harbour setting! Whether or not this is indeed true, Melbourne has ensured that it is the nation's sporting capital by establishing such great sporting events as the Melbourne Cup and Australian Open, amongst other leading annual events.

The footy

You can't escape the AFL (Australian Rules Football) in Melbourne as it's home to the most obsessive fans in the country. To us Brits it's a strange sport but to many Aussies it's a way of life.

The Melbourne Cricket Ground (MCG) is regarded as the 'spiritual' home of Aussie Rules.

From February to September AFL teams fight it out to make the top eight and qualify for the final series. As with football in the UK, both home and away games are played and there are championships. It might not be everyone's cup of tea but it's definitely worth a trip to a game as the atmosphere is electric and it's a great experience to share with friends. (www.melbournefc.com.au)

Commonwealth Games 2006

In 2006 Melbourne is home to the prestigious Commonwealth Games. The Melbourne 2006 Commonwealth Games will be a landmark in Melbourne's history, involving 4,500 athletes, representing 71 nations, ensuring that the city's reputation for hosting huge international events is set to continue.

Tennis

In January, the Australian Open attracts the *crème de la crème* of international players and every year over half a million spectators attend the matches, played over a fortnight, making it the most popular annual sporting event in Australia.

www.ausopen.com

Grand Prix

Petrol heads get their annual adrenalin fix over three days every March as the Grand Prix takes place in Melbourne's Albert Park.

www.grandprix.com.au

Horse racing

November marks the arrival of one of the most anticipated events on the sporting calendar, the Spring Racing Carnival. Melbourne comes alive for two weeks, during which time international visitors and locals get suited and booted and flock to the racecourse in Flemington to have a bet and enjoy a glass or two of champagne. The highlight of the Carnival is the famous Melbourne Cup where the entire city comes to a halt during the three-minute race. In fact most of Australia is caught up in the madness and offices usually join in with the obligatory sweepstake!

Golf

Lovers of the game should move to Melbourne! The city's 'sandbelt' is home to a host of championship courses, all within 20 minutes of one another, including Australia's most famous course, Royal Melbourne.

FOOD AND DRINK

Melbourne's dining is a reflection of its international and multicultural influences. Besides serving world-renowned Modern Australian cuisine, you will find many offerings from Asia, including Thailand, Vietnam and China, as well as familiar European dishes. Traditional Greek dishes are also frequently found on many menus. Due to the extensive fine wines that are made at nearby regions such as the Yarra Valley, there's sure to be a perfect wine to accompany your meal.

In March, Melbourne is host to the annual and hugely popular Food and Drink Festival which hosts over 100 mouth-watering events during 13 tasty days!

Restaurants

Fashionable, eclectic and sometimes eccentric – Melbourne's restaurants and cafés offer a dizzying spread of the world's great cuisines, serving long lunches and leisurely dinners. For waterfront dining, head down to the Southbank stretch of the Yarra River where you'll find plenty of cafés and restaurants offering great food and fabulous views. St Kilda is full of hip bars and fashionable restaurants but be sure to take your wallet!

For those with a sense of adventure, head out to the suburbs to explore one of Melbourne's specialist eating destinations – Richmond for cheap and cheerful Vietnamese dishes, Carlton for Italian classics, Fitzroy for tantalising Spanish tapas and of course Chinatown in the CBD for world class Chinese.

SHOPPING

Shopping in Melbourne is an eclectic affair – you can choose from large established department stores and big brand fashion boutiques or secondhand markets and discount outlets.

- Chapel Street has been a popular place for shoppers since before the First World War and is now home to 1,000 stores. It is *the* place to be seen and has established a reputation as Melbourne's style capital and the cutting edge of fashion and style. The South Yarra end has a distinctly up-market feel and is full of designer stores. The central Prahan strip is home to the big brand retailers, although Melbourne's up and coming young designers are increasingly choosing this location for launching new brands. It is also home to one of the city's premier fresh food markets. The lower end of Chapel Street is for the seriously cool and full of funky shops. The area comes alive after sundown with cosy lounge bars and buzzing bars full of Melbourne's young urban dwellers.

- Little Collins Street is a shopper's paradise and a great place to sample local designers' offerings. The area between Swanston and Elizabeth Streets is particularly known for great shoe shops.

- Toorak village's friendly and charming environment ensures that many locals and tourists flock to sample its exclusive fashion boutiques and local designer wear. It is one of the most exclusive and pleasant shopping areas in Melbourne.

Discount shopping

- Bridge Road in Richmond is the destination of choice for bargain hunters who make the most of the incredible bargains on offer there from leading retailers' warehouses.

- Sports enthusiasts should head to Smith Street in Collingwood which is brimming with factory outlets for top sporting brands such as Nike and Adidas.

VICTORIAN ATTRACTIONS

Victoria is a region of incredible natural beauty and has a wealth of attractions outside of Melbourne.

Geelong and the Bellarine Peninsular

Victoria's second largest city, Geelong, is only an hour's drive from Melbourne. Its sheltered waters make it a popular destination for swimmers, and the charming waterfront has many restored old buildings and many excellent cafés and restaurants. Along the western side of Port Philip Bay is the Bellarine Peninsula, which is a popular holiday spot for Melbournians. The seaside resort of Queenscliff is home to many glorious and extravagant old buildings and is also the centre for the peninsula's excellent dive scene.

Philip Island

Just over a 90-minute drive from Melbourne are the Philip Island Nature Parks. The parks are a haven for wildlife and the island's Penguin Parade is one the country's most popular and entertaining tourist attractions. The world's smallest penguins emerge from the sea and waddle ashore to their burrows for the evening, much to the pleasure of the hundreds of tourists waiting to witness this wonder. The area is thriving with native wildlife as well and you can take a tree-top walk through the bush to the Koala Conservation Centre to see Australia's favourite cuddly marsupial.

Great Ocean Drive

The Great Ocean Road hugs the contours of Victoria's rugged south west coast, taking visitors on one of Australia's greatest and most spectacular coastal drives. From Torquay to Nelson, the incredible road winds past scenic look-outs, takes you through vast rainforests and passes graveyards of ships lost at sea. The highlight is undoubtedly the Twelve Apostles, a unique group of 12 rock formations in the Port Campbell National Park that jut out of the sea.

Wine regions

There is a wealth of great wine regions to be found less than two hours' drive from downtown Melbourne including the Yarra Valley, Macedon Ranges and the Mornington Peninsular. There are 350 wineries in the area so be sure to get your taste buds ready for essential tastings to come!

USEFUL INFORMATION

British Consulate General: Level 17, 90 Collins Street, Melbourne. Tel: 1902 941 555 or 9652 1600.

23
Working and Studying in Victoria and Melbourne

In recent years Melbourne has established itself on the map as a global business centre. Conveniently located in the Asia Pacific time zone, Melbourne is ideally placed and Australia is the first market to open each day, providing a time zone bridge linking the closing of the US and the opening of the European markets. With half of the world's most expensive cities located in Asia, it offers an attractive alternative with a high quality lifestyle and competitive prices. Melbourne's economic and political centre is located within the municipal boundaries of the City of Melbourne, which includes the central business district and some of Melbourne's most historic suburbs and Southbank. The Port of Melbourne is Australia's largest container port, handling almost 40% of the nation's container trade as well as being one of the largest general cargo ports.

COST OF LIVING

Melbourne is less expensive to live in than its rival Sydney but more costly than the other capital States. However, salaries should reflect this and there is a wide range of affordable and decent accommodation. It also has a fantastic range of free outdoor activities to take advantage of.

QUALITY OF LIFE

Quality of life in Victoria is extremely high with the Economist Intelligence Unit ranking Melbourne No. 1 as the most liveable city in the world. In addition to its pleasant climate and multicultural society, Melbourne offers residents world-class educational facilities, modern and efficient transport networks as well as unlimited leisure possibilities. It is a safe, clean and cosmopolitan city to live in and it is easy to understand why so many migrants are attracted to starting a new life there.

The Grey Worldwide Eye (January 2005) survey on Australia shows that Melbournians are the most content in the nation, with 63% satisfied with their life, compared with just 50% of Sydneysiders and a national average of 56%. 'The results show that Melbourne offers a less stressful environment than Sydney – it's easier to get around, the pressures of mortgages are less and we have more time to spend with family and friends.'

(Source www.melbourne.vic.gov.au)

EMPLOYMENT OPPORTUNITIES FOR MIGRANTS

'The State Government of Victoria has set a population target of six million people by 2025, and attracting skilled and business migrants to fill shortages will play an important role in meeting this aim'.

Steve Bracks, Premier of Victoria

Skilled and business migrants are warmly welcomed to Victoria.

If your occupation is on the Victorian Skills in Demand List they may be able to help you move to this State via the Regional Skilled Migration scheme. You can check out the latest list of occupations in demand and further information at: www.liveinvictoria.vic.gov.au

Readers should note that within the metropolitan Melbourne area there is not a huge shortage of skilled workers, so it is unlikely that you would be able to migrate to the city under the Regional Skilled Migration visa. This scheme is in place to tempt workers into areas of the country where they are needed and these are usually outside of the major cities. However, you may be able to migrate under the Skilled Working Visa option.

To find out if your skills are in demand in Victoria click on to the Working in Victoria section of the above website.

At the time of writing this book, occupations in demand in Melbourne included mechanics, child care workers, civil engineers, medical staff and chefs.

MAIN INDUSTRIES

Victoria's great industry strengths are in agriculture, food, manufacturing, medical research, financial services, tourism and cultural industries. It is also Australia's leader in the new, knowledge-based industries such as information and communication technology, biotechnology, professional services, design, advanced manufacturing and environmental management.

Victoria's growth industries include:

- Information and communication technology (ICT). World-class research and development facilities and a highly ICT-literate domestic market have positioned Victoria as the ideal investment location for many ICT multinationals.

- Automotive. From design through to manufacture of cars, trucks and buses, Victoria accounts for almost 60% of Australia's $10 billion automotive industry.

- Biotechnology. Victoria is home to the largest biotechnology company base in Australia.

- Manufacturing. Victoria accounts for almost one-third of Australia's total manufacturing output.

- Financial services. Close to half of Australia's financial services industry providers are located in Melbourne.

- Food. Victoria accounts for 82% of Australia's dairy exports, and 52% of its processed fruit and vegetable exports. For more information, go to www.food.vic.gov.au

EDUCATION

For detailed information about education in Victoria refer to the following government site which is specifically written with migrants in mind: www.immi.gov.au/settle/education/vic.htm

School is compulsory in Victoria from the ages of 6 to 15. School goes from Prep to Year 12. Primary school lasts seven years and secondary school for six.

Primary

Children can attend school if they turn 5 by 30 April in the year they want to enrol. Primary school goes from Prep to Year 6.

Secondary

Secondary students study towards gaining their Victorian Certificate of Education (VCE). Students must obtain their VCE if they want to gain entry to university. The VCE is very competitive and entry marks for Victorian universities have been consistently high over recent years. Secondary education places emphasis on core areas of study whilst also encouraging students to concentrate on areas which are of particular interest.

Universities

Each year more than 150,000 students (50,000 international students live in Melbourne alone) choose to study in Australia. Internationally Melbourne has an enviable reputation as a centre of learning and is now considered one of the education capitals of Asia Pacific.

Victoria offers first degree education through to post-graduate levels of study through nine universities situated in and around the city. Students will need to have gained the VCE or equivalent to gain entry.

University of Melbourne

www.unimelb.edu.au

Founded in 1853, the University of Melbourne is now world renowned as the pinnacle of higher education in Australia.

Childcare

There are plenty of options regarding childcare in Victoria and Melbourne. Refer to www.google.com.au and search for options in your chosen areas.

24
Living in Brisbane and Queensland

State: Queensland – 'The Sunshine State'
Size: 1,727,000 sqm
Capital: Brisbane
Population: 1.6 million
Time zone: +10 GMT
Telephone area code: +61 7

QUEENSLAND

Queensland is the most northern state on Australia's east coast with a landscape ranging from vast outback deserts to lush topical rainforests and the coral blue reefs of the world famous Great Barrier Reef. It's affectionately called Australia's 'Sunshine State' and has an unbelievable average of 300 days of sunshine a year! Queensland is home to 3.95 million people, taking up around 25% of the continent's area.

Spectacular locations, beautiful weather and warm hospitality combine to make Australia's fastest growing State its most popular holiday State for both local and international visitors. Queensland offers activities for everyone, and hot spots include Surfers' Paradise, Brisbane, Cairns, the spectacular Great Barrier Reef and the tropical rainforests of the Daintree.

For more information refer to Queensland's tourism site: www.tq.com.au

BRISBANE

Brisbane has developed from a sleepy city that you passed en route to the Gold Coast to a world-class cosmopolitan centre. It is currently the third most populated city in the country and is the fastest growing. The heart of the city flows around the Brisbane River, and the balmy climate combined with the endless natural beauty, outdoor cafés and lush gardens make it a most appealing capital to live in.

Brisbane's interesting heritage and unique lifestyle have ensured that it is continuously evolving. Like many other Australian cities, because of the favourable climate the focus is on the outdoors and there are over 1,700 parks to enjoy.

Known to many of the locals as Bris Vegas, the city of Brisbane is a jungle of cultural activities and attractions. The arts capital of Queensland, Brisbane has dozens of theatres, cinemas, concert halls, auditoriums, galleries and museums. It is also is well known for its great cuisine with its abundance of fabulous seafood restaurants. The city has a mix of old and new buildings and offers nightlife that is rich in culture.

THE HISTORY

Brisbane has a colourful history and rich heritage. The then Governor of New South Wales (1821–1825), Sir Thomas Macdougall Brisbane, sent an exploration team north of Sydney with the task of finding a suitable location for a new penal settlement where they could send the very worst felons. They were required to find an area that could be reached by sea, which was the only means of long distance transport at that time, therefore a river location would be ideal. The site they found was named after the Governor and Brisbane was born. The penal settlement was abandoned in 1839 and the area was thrown open to free settlers in 1842.

As Queensland's huge agricultural and mineral resources were developed, Brisbane grew into a prosperous city, and in 1859 the state of Queensland separated from the colony of NSW. Brisbane was declared its capital. Today it is a fun and modern city and the envy of all Australia!

THE PEOPLE

The population is culturally diverse and more than a quarter of Brisbane's residents were born overseas. In 1996 over 15% of the population spoke a language other than English at home, with Cantonese, Italian, Vietnamese, Mandarin, Greek, Spanish, German, Polish and Russian being some of the most commonly spoken languages. Brisbane's rapid economic growth, its climate and wealth of facilities and resources have all attracted a massive wave of international migration. In the past 25 years, the State has also attracted over half a million Australians from other States to choose Queensland as their new home.

Brisbane is a youthful city with many young professionals attracted by the lifestyle, and who can blame them?

THE CLIMATE

Brisbane averages seven hours of sunshine daily (one of the highest ratings in the world). The average temperatures during the summer months hover at around the 30°C mark – but the city of Brisbane does experience a few much hotter days during summer. Brisbane's winter is very mild and quite pleasant in contrast to some of Australia's other States. The temperatures during winter generally remain around 17°C. Sea temperatures range from about a pleasant 26°C in summer to a moderate 19°C in winter so all year round swimming is possible.

THE CULTURE

Brisbane is an exciting cultural feast with a rich array of festivals, celebrations and exhibitions throughout the year. Brisbane is a cosmopolitan city that plays host to a variety of local, state, national and international events.

With annual cultural events such as the Brisbane International Film Festival and Brisbane's biggest annual festival, the spectacular River Festival, there is always something exciting happening along the beautiful Brisbane city skyline. Witness Queensland's largest and most magnificent pyrotechnic event at the Brisbane Riverfest's Riverfire.

THE ATTRACTIONS

Brisbane is home to many traditional and modern landmarks. Some are Queensland icons and others have great significance for specific heritage, sport and residential aspects.

Story Bridge

This impressive Brisbane landmark is one of Australia's finest bridges and is a historical landmark. Built in the early 1940s to link the city with Kangaroo Point, its construction was a triumph of local ingenuity. Sixty years on, it has become a major tourist attraction for visitors who wish to climb it!

The Gabba

Brisbane's most prized sporting venue and home to many of Australia's largest cricket matches. Many consider it hallowed turf.

South Bank

A short stroll from the CBD is the South Bank Parklands – a popular leisure destination since the site was host to the World Expo held in Australia in 1988. Home to the city's only man-made beach, the South Bank has become a mecca for locals and visitors to Brisbane. It's a great place for a picnic, a stroll or ride along the river front. You can shop, take in a movie or dine at one of the great restaurants. The Queensland Museum, Performing Arts Complex, State library and Brisbane Convention and Exhibition Centre are also all located around South Bank. On hot summer days in Brisbane, the South Bank is the place to be.

To find out more on the South Bank and forthcoming events check out:

www.south-bank.net.au

Roma Street Parkland

Located in the heart of Brisbane is the 'world's largest subtropical garden in a city centre'. This beautiful park is home to many unique plant specimens including 350 palms. It is free to visit and has seating, barbeque facilities and a subtropical rain forest. Climb aboard the *Jelly Bean Express* for a 15 minute trackless train ride around the various parkland habitats which show off the variety of landscapes seen within Queensland.

www.romastreetparkland.qld.gov.au

Little Stanley Street

Dine *al fresco* at one of the many eateries along bustling Little Stanley Street, opposite South Bank Parklands. Little Stanley Street is also home to South Bank Arts and Crafts Markets that operate from Friday evening until Sunday afternoon. You can also find the best fashion boutiques, accessories, gifts and homewares.

Queensland Performing Arts Centre

Opera and theatre lovers should check the local papers for details of current performances at the Optus Playhouse, Lyric Theatre, Concert Hall and Cremorne Theatre. These venues are all part of the Performing Arts Centre complex.

Tangalooma Wild Dolphin Resort

Located on the sheltered western side of Moreton Island, this popular resort is one of the few places in the world where you are allowed to interact with wild dolphins. A variety of accommodation is available, and tours of the island and water sports, such as sailing and windsurfing, are popular. Fast cat ferry services operate daily from the Holt Street Dock, off Kingsford-Smith Drive, Brisbane.

SHOPPING

Brisbane is a contemporary and stylish city and its shopping reflects this. Combining the unique and eclectic style that epitomises Brisbane there is a variety of popular shopping stores and boutiques spread throughout the city.

The central shopping precinct, the Queen Street Mall, is a shopper's paradise. There are also malls located in the Brisbane centre, Chinatown and Fortitude Valley. For more designer shopping boutiques stroll along Milton's Park Road or pop into the cosmopolitan New Farm or head to opulent Paddington for some antique shopping.

Late night shopping in Brisbane shopping centres outside the CBD is every Thursday night until 9pm. Shopping in the Queen Street Mall is extended till late every Friday night with most shops staying open until 9pm. On Friday nights you can also head over to Brisbane's South Bank for the night market extravaganza.

FOOD AND DRINK

Since the mid-1990s Brisbane has undergone a gastronomic revolution. It is now home to some of the finest restaurants and most innovative chefs in the country. As Brisbane is a large city with cultural diversity, the range of foods on offer will satisfy even the most exotic of taste buds. There is a wealth of great restaurants along the river and all year-round *al fresco* dining is possible due to the amazing climate. Seafood is particularly good in Brisbane and well priced, thereby ensuring that everyone can afford to eat out regularly, which they tend to do!

GETTING AROUND

Brisbane has a comprehensive public transport network in place combining train, bus and ferries. The Pacific Motorway carries the heavy traffic between Brisbane and the Gold Coast. Modern, efficient bus ways and rail links make getting around Brisbane and its surrounds easy and affordable.

Buses

Brisbane's buses are yellow and green, except for the City Circle bus which yellow and blue. They operate in and around the city and its suburbs.

If you just want to travel around the centre hop on the City Circle Bus (number 333), which travels clockwise along George, Brisbane, Wharf, Eagle, Mary, Albert and Alice Streets during the daytime on weekdays. It's a good way to see the sights and get your bearings.

Brit tip

For value for money purchase a Day Rovercard which gives unlimited travel for a whole day.

Ferries

The City Cat ferry operates a service along and across the Brisbane River with numerous stops at all key destinations. A one-way trip is currently $1.20 and ferries run every 10-15 minutes from dawn until after 11pm Monday to Saturday, with shorter hours on Sunday.

Trains

Citytrain is Brisbane's suburban rail provider running from the city centre out in all directions including Gympie and the Gold Coast. It is an easy and efficient way to get around without any worry. Trains run frequently to all areas, providing passengers with air-conditioned comfort.

Taxis

Yellow Cabs (13 19 24) and Black and White Cabs (13 10 08) are the two officially recognised services for Brisbane and surrounding areas.

A GUIDE TO BRISBANE'S SUBURBS

Brisbane has preserved and developed 'village areas', each possessing its own unique character. Leafy, hilly, suburbs surround the inner city, metropolitan Brisbane.

Popular suburbs

The Valley

North east of the CBD is the trend-setting Fortitude valley, or 'The Valley' as it is known locally, and is home to many young urban professionals. This area has become Brisbane's hippest area with contemporary heritage-style buildings mixed with edgy new cafés, bars, restaurants and nightclubs. The achingly cool Brunswick and Ann Street strips are the first choices for fashion conscious shoppers. This is also the location of Brisbane's Chinatown, adding to the culturally diverse blend of the area.

Paddington

North west of the city is Paddington – a cosmopolitan suburb and sought after residential area with many Queenslander homes set amongst lush gardens and leafy streets. It is also a popular meeting place, particularly at weekends, with locals enjoying its many boutiques, delis, galleries, restaurants, bars and clubs.

New Farm

West of the city is leafy New Farm, a vibrant suburb which is home to a large migrant population. It has many examples of ornate Victorian and 1930s style buildings, and this culturally diverse area has many great outdoor cafés, bars and eateries.

Kangaroo Point

Kangaroo Point forms a thin peninsula across the river from Brisbane CBD. It is close to the city but far enough away to feel a million miles from it. There are plenty of great apartment blocks and very expensive townhouses.

Bretts Wharf/Hamilton

This wharf is situated at the leafy and increasingly cosmopolitan waterfront suburb of Hamilton. It is only a short walk to the trendy cafés, restaurants and shops of Racecourse Road.

West End

Located in Brisbane's Outer South West End is arguably its most ethnically diverse suburb, with a large Greek, Irish, Cypriot and Lebanese population. There has been a recent gentrification of this area but it retains a bohemian charm.

For further information on Brisbane's suburbs refer to: www.ourbrisbane.com/living/suburbs

RENTING A HOME IN BRISBANE

Typically, houses in Queensland are large and generally situated on spacious suburban blocks ideal for gardens and outdoor activities. Queenslander style homes will become a familiar sight and are recognisable by their corrugated iron roof, weatherboard walls and sprawling verandas. They are often set high on stumps or poles.

Housing is affordable for most Queenslanders with Brisbane still offering cheaper housing options than other Australian cities.

*   www.rentalhotline.com.au is a Specialist Residential Property Management network, which covers the Brisbane area.

Other property sites:

*   www.ourbrisbane.realestate.com.au

*   www.couriermail.news.com.au

CHILDCARE

*   The Child Care Services Search facilities enable you to search for and locate childcare or early education services in Queensland: www.families.qld.gov.au/childcare

*   Playgroup Queensland offers a good opportunity for parents and their children to play, learn and have fun together. Call Playgroup Queensland on 1800 171 882 for more information.

QUEENSLAND ATTRACTIONS FURTHER AFIELD

Surfers' Paradise

Busy Surfers' Paradise, just an hour's drive from Brisbane, lies at the heart of the Gold Coast, a string of seaside towns spreading for 70 km from Beenleigh to Coolangatta on the New South Wales border. The action is centred around the shopping precincts of Cavill Avenue and the excellent surf beach. An evening craft market is held along the Esplanade on Friday nights. There are plenty of good places to eat, including glamorous restaurants and the many beachside cafés. At night the pubs and nightclubs are popular.

Tropical North Queensland

Cairns

Cairns is a modern tropical city with a relaxed atmosphere and is the primary gateway to the Great Barrier Reef region. Cairns is an ideal base to explore the wider Tropical North Queensland region, with front door access to the World Heritage listed reef, rainforest and outback. An amazing 600 tour options are available each and every day from Cairns.

The outback

Outback Queensland spans more than 830,000 square kilometres and is what many people consider the 'real' Australia. Rich in Australian heritage, fossilised history and Aboriginal art, it is thought to hold countless secrets. The world's oldest surviving culture, the Aboriginal people have existed in the region for over 60,000 years. Footprints of dinosaurs can still be found in rocks of the semi-desert regions.

Whitsunday's/Great Barrier Reef

The Whitsunday's region alone includes over 70 Great Barrier Reef islands. The Tropical North has even more.

Airlee beach marks the gateway to the outer barrier reef, which is possibly the world's most visually stunning holiday destination. Just one glimpse of its endless, crystal clear waters will explain. The Great Barrier Reef is the world's most complex reef system, stretching more than

2,000km along Queensland's northeast coast. It is made up of countless coral reefs and many surrounding islands, some of which are holiday resorts. These range from the family friendly Daydream Island to the exclusive playgrounds of the rich and famous which include Hayman and Hamilton Island Resort. There are many ways in which tourists can enjoy the reef. You can take a boat trip out for the day and island hop, or join one of the cruises that sail round the islands for between two and five days.

The coloured coral expanses just below the surface of the warm, crystal clear tropical waters are home to an unbelievable array of sea life. You can scuba to the deeper recesses, snorkel just below the dazzling surface, or view the watery wonderland from semi-submersibles and stay bone dry. Turtles, dolphins and manta rays are common sights to be enjoyed.

25
Working and Studying in Brisbane

COST OF LIVING

Brisbane is one of the more affordable capital cities in Australia in which to live. Accommodation costs are less than in Sydney and Melbourne and compare more favourably with the other capital cities. The costs of transport, food and entertainment are average for Australian cities. As Brisbane is a large and diverse multicultural city, there is a broad spectrum of living styles available and the city can be enjoyed even on even the smallest budgets.

Queensland's tax advantages

Queensland has one of the lowest State tax regimes in Australia.

Figures released by the Australian Bureau of Statistics in April 2004 reveal that Queenslanders pay approximately $1,867 per head in tax per annum, making Queensland the second lowest taxed State in Australia. New South Wales is the highest taxed State in the country at approximately $2,477 per head.

PROFILE

The central business district is dominated by corporate and public sector employment. Health is also a major employer, with the Royal Brisbane and a number of other hospitals located in the region. The occupations that employ the greatest numbers in the region are: sales assistants, computing professionals, general clerks, project and programme administrators, government administration, education workers, and legal and financial professionals.

Tourism

Queensland isn't called the Sunshine State for nothing. The source of much of Queensland's wealth is the tourist industry and this trend is set to continue as the State's popularity with both local and international visitors continues to grow. In fact, tourist dollars account for one in every ten dollars spent in Queensland due to the fact that many of the country's most impressive tourist attractions are located in this huge region. Its vast landmass also sustains other industries from sugar cane growing to mining.

EMPLOYMENT OPPORTUNITIES FOR MIGRANTS

Regional Queensland

There are good opportunities for skilled foreign workers in regional Queensland and you may be able to migrate via the Skilled Independent Regional Visa scheme. The Queensland government currently offers sponsorship under the Skilled Independent Regional visa for highly skilled and educated individuals who wish to live and work in regional Queensland.

Brisbane

However, this *does not* apply to those seeking to live and work in the metropolitan area of Brisbane, therefore you will need to apply via a different visa scheme such as Independent Skilled Migration. Check the DIMIA website for further details to see if your occupation/skills are currently in demand to meet the different visa types.

The following statement was sourced from the official website for local government in Queensland: www.sdi.qld.gov.au

Queensland Government Position Statement on Skilled Migration

The Queensland Government recognises and values the positive economic and social contribution that skilled migrants have made and will continue to make to the Smart State.

The Queensland Government encourages skilled migrants to settle in the State and will coordinate and develop support mechanisms that ensure skilled migrants and their families are welcomed, and that their positive impact on Queensland is maximised.

Queensland's clear commitment to skilled migration is clearly good news for those seeking to live and work in the Sunshine State.

INDIVIDUAL SKILLED MIGRATION

The Queensland government seeks to assist skilled migrants seeking work in regional areas in the following ways:

- They work with local governments, community organisations and employers interested in skilled migration.

- They use the skill matching database to ensure that details are available to employers in regional or low population growth areas who are looking to fill skilled vacancies.

- They offer post-arrival services available to successful migrants.

Refer to www.sdi.qld.gov.au

For further information on migration to Queensland:

- General Immigration Enquiries: Principal Migration Consultant: Phone: + 61 7 3224 8576.

- Business Migration: General enquiries: Phone: + 61 7 3224 2114.

- Individual Skilled Migration: Gen enquiries: Phone: + 61 7 3224 2075.

STARTING YOUR JOB SEARCH

www.qld.gov.au

It's worthwhile checking out the Queensland government site. It has a section on jobs and working and also provides helpful tips and advice for job seekers.

Centrelink Brisbane
Career Information Centre
340 Adelaide St
Brisbane 4001

Freephone: 1800 627 175
Fax: (07) 3000 4849

Local newspaper

The *Courier Mail* lists a large number of part-time/casual vacancies. Check on Wednesdays and Saturdays. Unfortunately you can't access their classifieds online.

Recruitment agencies

There are literally hundreds of recruitment and temping agencies in Brisbane. If you search the *Yellow Pages* for 'recruitment agencies' and then check the advertisements, they will list the areas that they cover (ie, hospitality, clerical, labour hire) to help you narrow your search.

Websites

* www.bluecollar.com.au This site contains useful information about wages in Queensland and also has a list of current vacancies in Brisbane and surrounds.

* www.mycareer.com.au/jobs-in/brisbane

* www.workplace.gov.au

EDUCATION

Children in Queensland are required to attend school from age 5 to age 15. All state schools are mixed sex. The school year is divided into two semesters and usually runs from late January to mid-December. There are two terms in each semester, with holiday breaks for Easter, winter, spring and summer. In Queensland every child is guaranteed enrolment at its local state primary school.

www.education.qld.gov.au

Enrolling in school

When you enrol your child in any school you will need to take proof of the child's date of birth, such as the child's birth certificate, passport or visa. Contact the school direct to get the necessary forms.

Primary/Preschool

Primary schools cater for children from Years 1 to 7 and preschools are provided for 4 and 5 year olds; however, this is non-compulsory. Both schools are usually housed under the same roof and will have the same principal. All students of this age study a curriculum which is the same throughout the state.

Secondary

Students enter secondary school at Year 8. They must, by law, stay at school until they are 15 years of age. Students may then choose to continue their Year 11 and 12 studies. Students wishing to continue to university must complete Year 12.

Before school, after school and vacation care

Some schools have formal centres attached to them which provide care for the children outside school hours. It is best to call individual schools to find out if they offer a service, and their costs and operating times.

TAFE (technical and further education)

For a guide of TAFE in Queensland refer to: www.tafe.qld.gov.au

Universities

There are nine well-respected universities in Queensland.

26
Living in Perth and Western Australia

State: Western Australia (WA) – 'The Wildflower State'
Size: 2,500,000 sqm (33% of the continent)
Capital: Perth
Population: 1.2 million
Time zone: + 8 hrs GMT
Telephone area code: + 61 8

WESTERN AUSTRALIA

Western Australia (WA) covers one-third of the Australian continent and is arguably the largest state in the world. It spans over 2.5 million square kilometres, and extends into different climatic zones simultaneously. Bordered largely by desert to the east, Western Australia is bounded by 12,500 kms of the world's most impressive coastline to the west.

Western Australia is famous for its brilliant blue skies, warm sunny climate and white sandy beaches, and is home to some of the world's most precious natural phenomena including the dolphins of Monkey Mia, the 350-million-old Bungle Bungle range and the remarkable Pinnacles Desert. Western Australia has a wealth of natural resources including gold, diamonds, iron ore, gas and minerals. Sophisticated yet uncomplicated, the WA lifestyle is relaxed and friendly, much like the rest of Australia!

The population of Western Australia is around two million people. It is divided into five regions: the Kimberley, the North West, South West, the Interior, and the Wheat Belt. The majority of the population lives along the beautiful white sandy beaches of the WA coast.

In 2002-2003 over 12,000 migrants settled in WA, representing around 13% of the total migrant intake to Australia. Migrants from the United Kingdom made up 27% of this total (source – DIMIA Immigration Update 2002-2003).

www.westernaustralia.com

PERTH

Perth is Western Australia's capital city and the major gateway into the state. It is one of the most isolated capital cities in the world. Geographically it is closer to South East Asia than it is to the east coast of Australia and it is in the same time zone as Hong Kong and Malaysia. It is in fact closer to Singapore than Sydney and its nearest neighbour of any size, the South Australian capital Adelaide, is 2,000 kilometres away.

Perth City is situated between the Darling Ranges and the Indian Ocean, and along the banks of the Swan River, only 12kms from the sea. It has a rapidly growing population and is a popular city for Australians to relocate to. It also attracts many Brits to its shores, lured by its Mediterranean climate offering warm to hot summers and cool, wet winters. The afternoon sea breeze (known as the Fremantle Doctor) offers relief to coastal towns during the summer.

Perth is a beautiful city which prides itself on its broad cultural diversity and it welcomes visitors to its city with open arms. It has modern facilities and an advanced transport system which allows commuters to travel on either buses or trains for free within a free transit zone in the city. Compared with Melbourne and Sydney, the city centre is on the small side and has just four major streets running east to west – St George's Terrace, Hay Street, Murray Street and Wellington Street, ensuring it's easy to get around.

Perth offers its residents a wonderful standard of life and is regarded by Australians as the perfect place for both families and young professionals. It has also become an increasingly popular tourist destination for overseas visitors in recent years and this trend is set to continue, which is having a positive effect on the local economy.

The city centre looks out over the broad stretches of the Swan River estuary (the river took its name from the famous black swans which can be found in its waters). The Swan hosts a range of water sports, including sailing, water skiing, sail boarding, jet boating, fishing, parasailing and cruising. There are more than 50 kilometres of riverside pathways for walking and cycling.

THE HISTORY

Australia's first inhabitants were Aboriginals and Torres Strait Islanders. They are believed to have arrived in migratory waves from South East Asia between 40,000 and 150,000 years ago, making Australia one of the oldest continents in the world both geologically and in terms of continuous human history.

The first recorded sighting by Europeans of Western Australia was in October 1616, when Dutch navigators landed at Shark Bay. British authorities settled at the Swan River in 1828 and, in 1829, Commander Captain Charles Fremantle raised the British flag at the head of the Swan River and claimed possession of the territory. A month or so later more British fleets arrived with settlers in tow and Perth was founded at a site near the present town hall on 12 August 1829.

WA was the last colony to join the federation of States that became the Commonwealth of Australia in 1901.

THE CLIMATE

Climate varies greatly in different parts of WA because the state covers such a vast area. Perth is famous for its sunshine with an average of eight hours a day. It has warm to hot summers and cool, wet winters. Its hottest month is February, when the maximum temperature averages 30 degrees.

THE CULTURE

Despite the fact that it is the most remote city in the world, Perth boasts the oldest international annual multi arts festival in the Southern Hemisphere. The Perth International Arts Festival launched in 1953, six years after the first Edinburgh Fringe Festival. The yearly event attracts around 300,000 people who flock to WA to see international and contemporary drama, theatre, music, film, visual arts, street arts, literature, comedy and free community events over a three-week period.

Throughout the rest of the year, you can find a wealth of cultural activities in Perth. The West Australian Opera performs six to nine weeks per year at the Edwardian His Majesty's Theatre. Ballet, dance and musical productions are also performed throughout the year at this beautiful venue. Film fans can catch the latest movies at many cinemas throughout the city and lovers of arthouse can catch a flick at Cinema Paradiso in Northbridge.

Although it does not have an iconic focal point such as the Sydney Opera House, the Perth Cultural Centre in Northbridge, which comprises the Art

Gallery, Perth Institute of Contemporary Arts and the Western Australian Museum, is well worth a visit.

THE ATTRACTIONS

Kings Park and Gardens

Set high on Mount Eliza, offering breathtaking views of the river and city, Kings Park comprises over 400 hectares of stunning parkland and greenery for people to enjoy all year round. In the summer, locals take advantage of the barbequing facilities and spend lazy days relaxing with the family. Others enjoy the recreational space available and run, cycle, roller blade or simply take a walk through the vast gardens. During certain times of the year special events are held including music festivals and the Australian Wildflower Festival. It is also becoming an increasingly popular venue for weddings.

Beaches

In the capital of Perth alone there are 19 pristine beaches, ensuring that even on a hot summer day (of which there are many) they never appear too busy or crowded. Come rain or shine, the surfers are in the water waiting for the perfect wave, and the seafront restaurants and cafés are brimming with locals enjoying brunch or a glass of wine after work. Not surprisingly, Perth is known as the Sunset Coast as, like the beaches, the sunsets are sensational and no two are ever the same. Perth's 35-kilometre coastline, stretching from Fremantle in the south to the northern suburbs, is easily accessible by the city's suburban bus and train network. The beaches are a major attraction to migrants seeking a taste of the fantastic lifestyle that Perth has to offer. Cottesloe is popular with families as it has many beachside cafés and City Beach has been voted one of the most beautiful in Perth by locals.

SPORT

As you will have realised by now there are few things that Aussies like more than watching sport or playing it (beer may be the only exception). Perth residents are not an exception to this rule.

Golf

Perth is blessed with numerous world-class golf courses – both private and public. The temperate climate means it is perfect weather for golf almost all year round, and many courses are located in natural settings featuring unique flora and fauna.

The footy

The Subiaco Oval is home to the local Australian Football League teams and games are played regularly throughout the season to capacity crowds. The State has two teams, The West Coast Eagles and The Fremantle Dockers.

On the water

With both the river and ocean on the doorstep, yachting, fishing, windsurfing and surfing are all hugely popular Perth pastimes. There are many local clubs and facilities to accommodate the growing demand.

Motorsports

The Telstra Rally is held annually in November in Perth, ensuring that petrol-heads get their adrenalin fix.

FOOD AND DRINK

Perth dining is a heavenly delight. It is a city of new taste sensations – a result of the influence that the large migrant population and the State's proximity to Asia have had on local menus and flavours. Dining out in Perth is all about fresh local produce, fine wines and a superb setting. There are endless cafés and restaurants, many offering *al fresco* dining. Japanese food has become increasingly popular and the availability of fantastically fresh seafood has led to many excellent sushi restaurants opening up across Perth. Of course you can wash down your meal with any number of premium Australian red and white wines.

Northbridge

This is the cultural and entertainment heartland of Perth. The buzzing, cosmopolitan suburb is the perfect place to sample the vast array of foods on offer and watch the endless streams of colourful people who flock to the area, all times of day and night. For years the area has attracted wave after wave of migrants, including Chinese, Greeks, Italians and more recently the Vietnamese. All of these have added to the diverse range of cuisine available at all ends of the budget. It really is the place to be, whether you fancy a chilled Sunday brunch with your family, or a lively Friday night drinks session with your friends – Northbridge offers something for anyone who wants to have a good time.

SHOPPING

Shopping in Perth is fun and affordable; however, it is more limited than Sydney and Melbourne in terms of range and diversity. There are two main shopping malls – Murray and Hay Street. Both offer a wide range of well-known high street stores and smaller boutique shops.

GETTING AROUND

Perth has a comprehensive and efficient public transport system and you can travel within the central city for free. For further information refer to: www.transperth.wa.gov.au

Buses

The Free Transit Zone (FTZ) allows you to travel on other buses within the City of Perth boundaries, without paying a fare. The Central Area Transit (CAT) services circulate specific routes every five to 15 minutes during the day, including Fremantle. Weekday services are more frequent than at weekends.

Perth has two major bus terminals. The Perth City Busport is located adjacent to the Perth Centre with frequent services to the Perth metro area including southern suburbs.

The Wellington Street Bus Station services routes to the northern suburbs.

Train

200ms down the road from Wellington Bus station is Perth Central Suburban Train Station. It has four main train lines, which cover all directions and service most main areas of Perth. The suburban trains are called Fast Track and are clean and efficient, offering a reliable service. Travel between City West and McIver is free because it is within the Free Transit Zones. All other destinations will require a ticket that must be purchased from a vending machine before boarding.

Brit tip

Always carry small notes (under $50) or change as you may find yourself unable use the ticket machine.

Interstate

The Indian Pacific Route is a famous train trip between Sydney, Adelaide and Perth. As the name implies, you pass two oceans on a journey that covers over 4,000kms and is a popular trip for tourists.

Ferries

The main ferry port in Perth is at Barrack Jetty, which transports passengers across the Swan River. They run regularly (approximately every 20 minutes) and are cheap and reliable.

Trams

An alternative travel option is Perth's trams, which offer a fun and traditional way of seeing the city's tourist attractions. You can hop on and off at your leisure. The tram stops are clearly marked and can be found throughout the city.

www.tramswest.com.au

Taxis

There are over 1,000 taxis operating in and around Perth.

- Swan Taxis tel: 13 1330 (within Australia)
- Black & White Taxis tel: 13 1008 (within Australia)

By bike

Perth's climate and its network of excellent trails make cycling a safe and enjoyable way to discover the city. Cyclists should note that you are required by law to wear bicycle helmet.

RESIDENTIAL GUIDE

Eastern region

Perth's eastern region is currently home to over 260,000 people; the region's population growth is forecast to be over 8% per annum over the next ten years. Residents come from diverse cultural backgrounds with over a third being born overseas, predominantly in European and Asian countries. This area offers a wonderful quality of life, and the vast natural attractions such as pristine national parks and the waterways of the beautiful Swan River are right on the region's doorstep.

Subiaco

Subiaco is a thriving village suburb, only seven minutes from Perth and 20 minutes from Fremantle. It has a unique character and charm, which has grown in popularity in recent years due to its proximity to Perth. It offers residents excellent shopping, restaurants and nightlife. Next to the train station you will find Subiaco Oval, home of Australian Rules football in WA that has recently been renovated to hold around 40,000 spectators.

www.subiacocity.com

Beach towns

Beach suburbs are among the most popular and they include Cottesloe, Trigg and Swanbourne.

Riverside suburbs

Riverside suburbs such as South Perth and Dalkeith are also popular. These are also among the wealthiest suburbs.

South Perth

South Perth offers residents some of the best views of the city from across the Swan River. With the Royal Perth Golf Course and Perth Zoo, and only minutes from the Perth CBD, South Perth is a very desirable suburb which has seen house prices go through the roof in recent years.

Dalkeith

The prestigious suburb of Dalkeith is arguably the closest prestige single residential suburb to Perth, just some 7 kilometres along the river, with Kings Park one side and the Swan the other. It has many attractive features including the Parklands Reserve and the beautiful White Beach, which is the widest strip of white sandy beach north of the river.

Joondalup

Renowned for its cosmopolitan outlook, Joondalup is fast becoming a very desirable place to live and its residential area is growing. It offers a laid back and leisurely style of living and is becoming increasingly trendy. Pubs, café-bars and restaurants are springing up everywhere. Its close proximity to the freeway and great local transport will ensure its continuing popularity.

www.joondalup.wa.gov.au

FINDING A PROPERTY

Prices

The average house price in Perth is now $240,000 (approximately £100,000), almost half the price of a home in Sydney, according to figures from the Real Estate Institute of Western Australia (REIWA).

Of course, prices will vary throughout suburbs to the north and south, with those overlooking the Indian Ocean being considerably more expensive.

In Perth you can buy or rent houses and home units (flats) direct from their owners as a private sale or through a real estate agent.

Local newspapers

The Sunday Times

This is the largest selling weekly newspaper in Western Australia and has a property section that includes rentals.

The West Australian

www.thewest.com.au

The website has a useful and detailed online rental property search tool and also has a comprehensive jobs section.

Other useful on-line property search tools

- www.realestateguide.com.au/location_western_australia.cfm
- www.perthexchange.com.au

CHILDCARE

www.careforkids.com.au is a comprehensive website that covers all of Australia and allows you to search for childcare options in your chosen area.

WESTERN AUSTRALIAN ATTRACTIONS

Fremantle

Fremantle, known locally as 'Freo', is just 20 minutes' drive from Perth city. It offers a charming alternative to the hustle and bustle of Perth, and its many galleries, shops, markets and museums ensure that it's a popular place to live. The ferry makes it accessible for commuters. Locals refer to the 'Freo feeling' which they say comes upon you when entering the area from the city and remains until you leave.

Rottnest

Rottnest Island, or 'Rotto', is half an hour's ferry ride from Fremantle, which makes it perfect for a day trip, or short escape from the city. The island is surrounded by many fine beaches and bays and is popular for water sports. As Rottnest is virtually traffic free thanks to a 'no visitors' cars rule', the most popular way to get around is by bicycle. Dolphins are a familiar sight around the Rotto area, but those seeking the ultimate marine experience head a few hours north of Perth to the crystal-clear blue waters of World Heritage listed Monkey Mia. Here, the bottle-nosed dolphins come into shore daily to feed and play with the many visitors who stand knee deep in water under the watchful eye of a ranger.

Broome

Broome is located on the Indian Ocean's doorstep at the South Western tip of Australia's last frontier of pristine wilderness, The Kimberly. It is known as the Pearl of the North in reference to the time when it was the pearling capital of the world, and pearling still remains a thriving business and its roots are evident thoughout the town.

From the cosmopolitan character of Chinatown to the endless white sands of Cable Beach and the red sandstone cliffs, Broome is a multicultural and breathtaking delight to visit.

Wineries

As with most State capital cities in Australia, wineries can be found in abundance around Perth and surrounding areas. Wine country can be found just 30 minutes' drive to the north of the city, where you can find yourself sipping the finest Chardonnays in the Swan Valley, which is the States' oldest wine region.

Three hours south of Perth is the beautiful Margaret River, which has gained a reputation for being one of Australia's premium food and wine regions. The area is renowned for its spectacular coastlines, limestone caves, and of course its wine, with many vineyards in the region offering tours and daily tastings to tantalise your taste buds.

USEFUL INFORMATION

- Local time in Perth is eight hours ahead of Greenwich Mean Time. Unlike all the other Australian States, Perth does not practise daylight savings.

- British Consulate
  Level 26, Allendale Square
  77 St Georges Terrace
  Perth
  Western Australia 6000
  Tel: (08) 9224 4700

27
Working and Studying in Perth

COST OF LIVING

Perth offers a quality of life and choice of lifestyle that are particularly attractive to both Australians and migrants. The region's growing population comes from diverse cultural backgrounds with over a third being born overseas, predominantly in European and Asian countries.

Western Australia consistently ranks as one of the best locations in the world for quality of life and also one of the more affordable.

The Mercer Study rated Perth as the cheapest Australian capital city – 126th on the worldwide list and also the safest (ranking 25th safest in the world).

CURRENT ECONOMIC OVERVIEW

Due to its location on the edge of the Indian Ocean and the vast distance from its Australian neighbours (not to mention the two-hour time difference between the east and west coast), Perth and Western Australia generally have formed close business links with Asia. While many developed economies have struggled in recent years to fight off recession, Western Australia's economy has been averaging growth rates of over 5% per annum for the past decade. It has also boasted the lowest average unemployment rates of all Australian states.

Top industries

There are many admin and IT opportunities in Perth. Other notable industries include finance, tourism, hospitals and nursing homes, government administration, teaching, legal and accounting services. Western Australia also has thriving mining and farming communities. With just 10% of the total population, Western Australia is responsible for a whopping quarter of all Australia's exports. Also of particular note is the Perth real estate industry, which is very buoyant and employs many people in building, renovating, selling and managing real estate.

EMPLOYMENT OPPORTUNITIES

Perth's workforce is skilled. Almost half possess post-secondary or tertiary qualifications and two thirds have completed the highest level of secondary education.

However, there are plenty of opportunities for skilled workers in WA and the Perth region, and the area is an incredibly popular migration destination for Brits. This trend seems set to continue as WA is enjoying prosperous times. You may be able to apply for a visa under the Regional Skilled Worker scheme as they are suffering some worker shortages. Check the Skilled Occupations List and Occupations in Demand List for this region on the immigration website ahead of your visa application.

At the date of writing, on the Australian job search website there were 2,000 job vacancies posted in the Perth area, half of which were in the city.

Unemployment

The trend unemployment rate in WA at January 2005 remained at 4.5% (source ABS). This was a decrease from January 2004 and is below the national average.

Starting your Perth job search

* www.jobs.wa.gov.au provides an online listing of jobs available across the Western Australian government, as well as other career-related information.

* www.thewest.com.au the *West Australian* is the local newspaper for this region. Their website has a useful online jobs section as well as providing good information about the area.

* www.jobsearch.gov.au is a government based website that lists positions available in Perth and surrounding areas. You can search by occupation.

* www.jobsinhealth.emhs.wa.gov.au As with many regions in Australia, WA and Perth are experiencing shortages in nursing staff. This site lists available positions across the local hospitals.

    www.positionsvacant.co.au

EDUCATION

Education is compulsory to the end of the school year in which the student turns 15 years of age. The Western Australian school education system is divided into three stages:

* pre-primary/pre-school education

* primary education

* secondary education.

Primary

Children may choose to attend pre-primary school education in the year they turn 5; however, it is compulsory for all children to start primary school in the year they turn 6 (year 1).

Primary school in Western Australia continues until Year 7.

Secondary

Secondary education starts at Year 8 and may continue to Year 12. By law, children must stay at school until the end of the year they turn 15; however, if they wish to gain entry to university they will need to continue their studies until Year 12. Should they complete Year 12 with satisfactory grades and gain the Western Australian Certificate of Education (WACE) they may continue on to uni.

University

The high quality of Western Australia's education system is recognised worldwide and attracts around 20,000 overseas students annually. Fees for courses in Perth are much the same as those in Melbourne and Sydney, but Perth's cost of living means students' dollars stretch further.

- Edith Cowan University:
  www.ecu.edu.au

- Murdoch University:
  www.murdoch.edu.au

- University of Western Australia:
  www.uwa.edu.au

28
Living in Adelaide and South Australia

State: South Australia (SA) – 'The Festival State'
Size: 984,000 sq km
Capital: Adelaide
Population: 1.1 million
Time zone: +9.5 GMT
Telephone area code: + 61 8

SOUTH AUSTRALIA

South Australia is the southern, central State on the mainland of the continent of Australia.

It has an area of nearly one million square kilometres and is the driest of the Australian States and Territories. The local population is dependent on water from the River Murray, the only major river in the State. It is the opal capital of the world.

South Australia boasts a diverse range of different landscapes from the Adelaide Hills surrounding the city to the grasslands and valleys of the Fleurieu Peninsula, to the Barossa Valley, or the semi-arid and arid deserts in the north of the State in places such as the Flinders Ranges. There is a marked distinction between the fertile, contained southern half of this state and the harsh, untamed desert of the north. Ninety-nine per cent of South Australia's inhabitants live in Adelaide, the park-blanketed capital on the fertile southern shoreline.

www.southaustralia.com

ADELAIDE

If the rest of Australia or any small part were half as beautiful it was a fortunate country.

Mark Twain, 1895

Adelaide is the capital city of South Australia and home to around 1.1 million people. Australia's only State capital not established with the use of convict labour, the city has a less commercial feel to it than some of the other capitals and is unspoilt by modern developments. It can be described as an elegant and preserved city which is rich in Aboriginal and European heritage. The wine and festival capital of Australia, Adelaide is one of the most vibrant, stylish and innovative cities in the Southern Hemisphere. It's a place to experience the buzz, culture and convenience of a big city without the frustrations. The city is a charming blend of historic buildings, wide streets, numerous shops, street cafés and restaurants. Currently it is home to a mix of young professionals and families who enjoy the many pleasures that this understated city has to offer. It is also becoming an increasingly popular destination for migrants.

It is often referred to as a 'city within a park' as it is surrounded by seemingly endless parklands. Designed by Colonel William Light, in his original plan of the city in 1837 the ring of parklands contains 29 parks and incorporates an incredible 45% of the city area. These areas of outstanding beauty and endless recreational opportunities are considered a prized asset to the city and are extremely well maintained. Each park has its own unique character: there are formal rose gardens, wide spaces with grand native and exotic trees, playgrounds and lakes, and numerous sporting fields which provide venues for a diverse range of sporting activities from archery to cricket. A range of landscapes surround the city, including the Mount Lofty Ranges and the white sandy beaches and the seas of Gulf St Vincent to the west. This pleasant mix creates a unique Australian city with one of the best city lifestyles to be found anywhere in the world. In the past Adelaide has also been known as the 'city of churches' for its large number of beautiful churches built by the early colonists.

It is divided into two parts, Adelaide and North Adelaide, separated by Torrens River which has been cleverly transformed into a beautiful recreational lake. North Adelaide is considered to comprise the more trendy and up-market part of the city. Adelaide airport is about 6km west of the city centre, and the interstate train terminal is just south-west of the city centre in the suburb of Keswick.

Rundle Street is Adelaide's cosmopolitan centre and a part of the historic East End of Adelaide. It's full of cafés, hotels, restaurants and small interesting shops. As well as the 40 or so eating outlets, it also has ten hotels, wine bars, a number of offices, around 100 shops and 11 cinema screens.

The East End is also pleasantly situated amongst a number of Adelaide's popular attractions, including the Botanical Gardens, Wine Centre, Rymill Park, Rundle Mall, and the many cultural highlights and heritage buildings along North Terrace.

THE HISTORY

The Kaurna people lived for many thousands of years in the Adelaide plains of South Australia. They were made up of independent groups living within their own lands but who came together for trade, social, ceremonial and religious reasons. The Kaurna people were pushed out of

Adelaide by the city's development.

Colonel William Light was the first Surveyor-General of South Australia. He arrived in South Australia in 1836, with the task of deciding upon the site for Adelaide. His survey began on 11 January 1837, at the northwestern corner of Adelaide, at the junction of North and West Terraces. The Newmarket Hotel is directly across the exact location on North Terrace.

THE PEOPLE

Adelaide is a multicultural city with a population made up of over 100 different ethnic communities. Many of these communities proudly maintain links with their culture. The city combines interest, creativity and liveliness with a safe and clean environment. South Australians lead a relaxed but exciting lifestyle, in a State with a rich history, and a particular love of fine wine and food. By evening and at the weekend, many take advantage of the weather and enjoy *al fresco* dining at one of the fine restaurants and cafés that give the city its cosmopolitan but casual feel.

THE CLIMATE

As with most other Australian cities, Adelaide enjoys a Mediterranean climate with warm, dry summers averaging 29°C and mild winters around a very pleasant 15°C. In fact it is the driest city in the driest state in the driest continent. Luckily for locals South Australia is also home to an incredible 4,000 kilometres of coastline and some of the country's most beautiful scenery with unspoilt beaches within an hour's drive of the city limits.

THE CULTURE

Adelaide is devoted to the worship of food, wine, culture and the arts. This enthusiasm has spawned a procession of events, culminating in the biennial three-week Adelaide Festival/Fringe Festival which takes place in late February/early March and comprises live drama, dance and musical events. There is also a writers' week, art exhibitions, and poetry readings, with guest speakers and performers from around the world. The Fringe Festival, about the same time, features alternative music and performance art. Other world-leading events include the Clipsal 500 (V8 supercar race), Jacob's Creek Tour Down Under (international cycling race), Magic Millions Carnival (racing horse sales) and the Royal Adelaide Show.

It is also the wine capital of Australia and an incredible six out of the top ten Australian wines are made within a few hours' drive of the city.

Many of South Australia's great cultural institutions are located on leafy North Terrace (also known as Adelaide's cultural boulevard). The State's library, museum, art gallery and the Migration Museum have pride of place alongside Parliament House, the University of Adelaide and Government House.

View the best collection of early Australian art in the country, and a highly significant collection of Aboriginal dot paintings of the Western Desert, at the Art Gallery of South Australia.

THE ATTRACTIONS

Adelaide Botanic Garden

Established in 1857, the 16 hectares of gardens are located on the North Terrace. A haven in the city, the gardens were established in 1857 and are home to more than 5,000 roses and a lush tropical rainforest housed in the Bicentennial Conservatory (which happens to be the largest glasshouse in the southern hemisphere). Free guided walks of the Botanic Garden are conducted by the Friends of the Botanic Gardens of Adelaide.

Festival Centre

The world famous Adelaide Festival Centre sits in Elder Park on the banks of the Torrens River. This impressive arts complex comprises a drama theatre, a lyric theatre, an open air amphitheatre and a multipurpose concert hall. The centre holds a diverse range of interesting cultural activities throughout the year and is widely regarded as one of the best live performance venues in the world.

Art Gallery of South Australia

Adelaide has always had a close association with the arts and the region has produced more than its fair share of significant Australian artists, all of whom are well represented and displayed in the Art Gallery. It is most well known for holding one of Australia's finest, largest and oldest public art collections.

SHOPPING

Adelaide is full of surprises and the fabulous shopping on offer often pleasantly surprises visitors.

Rundle Mall is the heart of shopping in the city, with international retail stores and trendy boutiques intertwined with cafés, elegant arcades and inspiring architecture.

To the east, the Mall becomes Rundle Street, Adelaide's cosmopolitan centre and part of the historic East End. This area is notorious for its great bars and restaurants and quirky fashion shops. To the west, Hindley Street has much-loved book and music shops tucked among quirky cafés and bars. Bargain hunters should head to Glen Osmond Road at Eastwood where you have your pick of top label fashion items at low prices.

King William Road at Hyde Park is great for boutiques, antiques and old wares, whilst Southbound shoppers can enjoy the convenience of undercover shopping at Westfield Shoppingtown Marion. To the east, Burnside Village is one of the most elegant shopping environments in Adelaide.

If you like to combine shopping with a trip to the beach then hop on a tram to the always busy Jetty Road at Glenelg which has a pleasant seaside precinct, not to mention a fabulous stretch of golden sand.

Adelaide's Central Market

If you enjoy the hustle and bustle of markets, then join the thousands who come to buy the superb local fresh produce and gastronomic delights from Southern Australia at Adelaide's Central Market. For over 130 years, it has been the place for locals to buy their fresh produce and many come just to enjoy the fun and friendly atmosphere. On Friday nights and Saturday mornings musicians often provide live entertainment. Nearby Chinatown is also great for fresh local produce and authentic Chinese food.

FOOD AND DRINK

Adelaide's residents and visitors have a lot to thank the South Australian government for, as in the 1970s they implemented a restaurants policy in an attempt to improve the standard of cuisine, and Adelaide was its primary target. The initiative was a great success and led to the city being regarded as the birthplace of modern Australian cuisine. The fabulous restaurants and cafés reflect the high standards that the city set itself and Adelaide is now a gastronomic delight, boasting more restaurants per person than any other city in Australia. There's no shortage of options covering a varied selection of cuisines, price range and styles. The nearby vineyards of Clare Valley and Barossa ensure that there is an excellent selection of fine wines to accompany any meal.

Each area of Adelaide has a distinct food personality. Stylish Rundle Street East is the place for *al fresco* dining and offers diners an eclectic mix of cuisines, including Greek, Thai, Japanese, Italian, and Malaysian, whilst Gouger Street at the famous Central Market is the place for seafood lovers. In North Adelaide, O'Connell and Melbourne Streets offer a great mix of fine dining and café society. Glenelg is always a popular destination for those seeking good food with a seaside view.

Not only is the standard of food very high in Adelaide, it's also very reasonable. When compared with other State capitals, food and wine prices are low and you can expect to pay a third less than at a restaurant of comparable style in Sydney or Melbourne.

The city's nearest wine cellars are a stone's throw away and Penfold's Magill Estate, the birthplace of Australia's most famous wine, Grange, is only 20 minutes' drive. Others close by include Angove's Winery at Tea Tree Gully and Dina Grilli's Primo Estate, which offer tastings of both their wines and award-winning olive oils.

SPORT

Adelaide residents have a keen interest in sport but are nowhere near as obsessed as those in other Australian cities.

A local footy team, the Adelaide Crows, play in the Australian Football League (AFL). You can catch them in action from March to September with all home games played at AAMI Stadium.

Due to the vast parklands in and around the city, there is a wealth of sporting facilities available, covering every type of activity you could wish for including: golf, walking, cycling, swimming, tennis, bowls and archery.

GETTING AROUND

Adelaide is regarded as Australia's '20-minute city', which stems from the fact that most people's daily commute is approximately this amount of time. How marvellous! This means that residents have more free time to spend on leisure pursuits, which is one of the great delights of living in Adelaide.

The city was clearly designed for the convenience of people and you can access the city centre from all parts of the metropolitan area. Almost everything is within walking distance of the central business district (CBD) as the city centre is on a grid system with most streets and squares within 1 square mile. The main street (King William Street) runs directly from north to south of the city through Victoria Square, which is at the heart of the city.

Adelaide also has an effective transport system. The Metro services the greater metropolitan region with trains and buses – and the Glenelg tram. Of particular note are the Adelaide free buses that cover the CBD. These bright yellow buses travel the main streets and go to the main attractions in the city. Trains connect the northern and southern suburbs with the city centre, and the railway station is in the city centre beneath the Casino and Convention Centre complex.

www.adelaidemetro.com.au

Brit tip

- The cheapest ticket is a two-section ticket, which allows you to make a single journey of approximately 3 kilometres. This ticket costs $2, or $1.50 between 9.00 and 15.00.

- The best value though is a one-day ticket. This can be bought on buses, trains and trams.

THE SUBURBS

Adelaide is a commuter's dream as a belt of parklands and beautiful leafy suburbs surrounds the city.

Adelaide Hills

Only 20 minutes from the heart of the city, Adelaide Hills is known for having gorgeous gardens, numerous vineyards, world-class attractions and great food. It is South Australia's most diverse and accessible region.

North Adelaide

North Adelaide is steeped in Australian history and features many heritage listed buildings. Local residents have featured in major events like the forming of the Australian Constitution and the birth of cricket in South Australia. The streets are wide and tree lined. There are two main shopping precincts, Melbourne Street and the Adelaide Icon. The Royal Oak Hotel about halfway along O'Connell Street is very popular and has musical entertainment with local bands. At the northern end of O'Connell there is the Art Deco style Piccadilly picture theatre.

West Adelaide

The inner western suburbs are lively and busy. From central Adelaide the bay tram travels 11 kilometres south west to Glenelg, Adelaide's earliest suburb and a popular beach resort. Along the western coastline are 30 sandy beaches.

South Adelaide

Immediately south of the city the up-market inner suburbs begin, with antique and designer fashion stores, as well as many restaurants. Further south there is a growing amount of housing commission developments.

East Adelaide

The inner eastern suburbs are Adelaide's cosmopolitan quarter, with a thriving restaurant and café society, as well as a sizable student contingent. The Adelaide Hills are only 20 minutes from the central city, and to the east are many small commuter suburbs.

The Torrens River

The Torrens River dissects the parklands in which the city sits and separates North Adelaide from Adelaide. Boat trips can be taken along the river and to the nearby Adelaide Zoo. There are waterside restaurants and pleasant riverside walks through expansive parklands.

Beaches

Adelaide has more than its share of great beaches, in fact 60km of white sandy beachfront makes up Adelaide's metropolitan coast. The beautiful sandy beaches of Adelaide play an important part in the lifestyle of local residents. Beaches stretch all the way down the coast from Semaphore in the north to Sellick's Beach in the south. Undoubtedly the most popular beach can be found at Glenelg.

Glenelg

Lying several kilometers to the west of the city are miles of white sandy beaches bordering the clear blue seas of Gulf St Vincent. Glenelg can be easily reached by the heritage tram ride from the city centre. Glenelg is Adelaide's equivalent of Sydney's Bondi Beach and is a haven for locals and tourists alike who come to enjoy the many activities on offer.

RENTING A HOME IN ADELAIDE

Adelaide offers a wide range of housing options that can satisfy all tastes and meet all budgets. The housing mix contains heritage and contemporary properties ranging from quaint 19th century cottages to terrace houses, villas and free-standing mansions besides contemporary flats, townhouses and warehouse apartments.

As you would expect, renting a home in Adelaide is cheaper than other Australian capital cities. For example a two-bedroom apartment rents for $180 to $250 a week compared with $215 to $300 a week in the eastern seaboard capital cities.

Adelaide's daily newspaper, *The Advertiser*, has classified advertisements from landlords and real estate agents: www.newsclassifieds.com.au

- www.adelaideexchange.com.au – homes and jobs

FURTHER AFIELD

Adelaide is also an easy gateway to the famous Aussie Outback, the dramatic Flinders Ranges, the natural beauty of Kangaroo Island, the River Murray and the many South Australian vineyards that produce some of the world's great wines.

Flinders Range and outback

The Flinders Range is a stunning mountain range which dates back over 600 million years. It covers 80% of South Australia but is home to less than 1% of the State's population. It is a land of extreme contrasts – from the wetlands of Coongie Lake to the pink parallel dunes of the Simpson Desert down. Aboriginal towns celebrate the history of the region and the art of the Aboriginal people is recorded at many sites, the best known at Yourambulla Caves. Much of the area is national park, and the extensive area of rolling hills of the Flinders Range National Park is home to many native Aussie animals including red kangaroo, emus and galahs. There are three deserts in the outback area, with vast dry salt lakes scattered around them. The discovery of opal in the outback resulted in the establishment of mining towns, most notably Coober Pedy, the largest opal-mining town in Australia. The Flinders Range attracts geologists and paleontologists from around the globe who are keen to uncover the hidden fossils that may hold the key to our evolution.

Wine country

South Australia is home to some of the best wine makers in the world. The regions of Barossa, Coonawarra, Adelaide Hills, McLaren Vale and Clare Valley allow you to experience the pleasures of the vines first hand and up close.

The region offers everything you'd expect from Australia's most famous wine area and all less than an hour from Adelaide. Grand chateaux surrounded by ornate gardens, picturesque villages provide great stop offs for those seeking delicious food and wine. There are also many regular festivals and events in the region such as the Hot Air Balloon Regatta each May, the Barossa Classic Gourmet showcasing restaurants and wineries in August, or the 16-day International Music Festival in October, amongst others.

Kangaroo Island

Visitors from all around the world come to Kangaroo Island for a true, unspoilt Australian experience. The third largest off-shore island in Australia it a nature lovers' dream and a third of the island consists of National Parks and Conservation Parks including five significant Wilderness Protection Areas. Kangaroo Island has an interesting history. Not surprisingly, there is abundant wildlife, much of which is uncommon or extinct on mainland Australia. Kangaroo Island was the first place in South Australia to be settled, in July 1836.

USEFUL INFORMATION

- Adelaide is 9.5 hours ahead of GMT.

- The South Australian Visitor and Travel Centre – City:
  18 King William Street, Adelaide. Opening hours: Monday–Friday
  8.30am–5pm. Weekends and public holidays 9am–2pm. Closed
  Christmas Day. Tel: 1300 655 276.

- For further information on SA, please refer to
  www.southaustralia.com

29
Working and Studying in Adelaide

COST OF LIVING

Adelaide is one of the least expensive cities in the world, according to a survey conducted by global economics consultants Mercer Consulting Group (source: Mercer, May 2004).

In Mercer's international annual cost of living survey, Adelaide regularly achieves an excellent ranking as one of the most affordable cities. Housing and rental costs are also lower in Adelaide than in most other modern cities of the world.

Adelaide is significantly less expensive than other Australian cities, particularly Sydney, Melbourne and Brisbane.

Although Adelaide can boast a lower cost of living than the eastern States, incomes are not proportionately lower. The city also offers a wonderfully high standard of living, all of which is good news for potential migrants.

CURRENT ECONOMIC OVERVIEW

Adelaide is the cultural, political and social epicentre of South Australia and in early 2004 was ranked the nation's most competitive business city by KPMG International.

Main industries

South Australia is a leader in the Australian food industry. It is the largest producer of quality lamb, has a flourishing fishing industry (a result of having the cleanest waters in the world), and is the source of fresh juices and sparkling mineral waters. It is also the most successful wine producing State, making about 50% of Australian wines and 65% of national wine exports.

Natural beauty, a temperate climate, and a thriving arts and cultural community combine to support the State's billion-dollar tourism industry.

The region has also established a reputation for excellence in electronics and defence related manufacture which accounts for a third of the nation's defence spending.

EMPLOYMENT OPPORTUNITIES

South Australia is a very tolerant society that welcomes migrants from all cultures. The State government actively seeks migrants, particularly those with skills which are needed to help ensure the ongoing development of the State, and business migrants.

Adelaide offers many and varied job opportunities in the private and public sectors across a range of thriving key industries which currently include healthcare, engineering, wine, automotive, manufacturing, defence, services, medical research and hospitality.

Skilled vacancies/shortages

The South Australian Immigration site has very useful information for potential migrants and has useful fact sheets which may help aid your decision process. You can also download a very helpful brochure on skilled migration: www.immigration.sa.gov.au

Adelaide is also one of the few capital cities in Australia that allows migrants to apply under the Skilled Independent Regional Visa scheme. This visa is generally only applicable to rural areas to encourage skilled workers out of the city and into the regions. However, as Adelaide is experiencing shortages in their workforce you may be able to apply via this route which allows those who do not meet the points required for Skilled Regional Migration the chance to secure a three-year work visa. For further information refer to the DIMIA website: www.immi.gov.au/facts/26state.htm

Looking for work

www.southaustralia.biz is a government site with invaluable and up to date information about:

- local economy

- jobs market

- cost of living

- lifestyle

- education

- moving to Adelaide

- business migration.

It also has useful links to other helpful sites.

EDUCATION

www.immi.gov.au/settle/education/sa.htm

All children between the ages of 6 and 15 years must attend school in South Australia. Non-residents must pay for their children's schooling and fees vary in each State. Private school fees in Adelaide are generally lower than those charged in most other Australian State capitals.

South Australia offers a very high standard of education through a wide range of government and private schools and colleges. Schools are well placed throughout Adelaide's metropolitan area and other towns and cities throughout the State and are easily reached by their students.

For further information on schooling for international students, entry requirements and a guide to the fees involved, log on to: www.internationalstudents.sa.edu.au

Primary

In South Australia children attend primary school from reception to Year 7. Reception is the first year of primary school and is where children are introduced to school life.

Secondary

Secondary courses are offered from Years 8–12. Senior secondary education, Years 11–12, is available to students who can choose a wide range of subjects to complete a South Australian Certificate of Education over a two-year period.

The normal entrance requirement for university courses is the South Australian Certificate of Education (SACE) with recorded passes in five subjects at Year 12, or the interstate or overseas equivalent.

Universities

Adelaide is a university city, with two of its three world-class universities located in the CBD. They provide a broad range of quality courses to more than 40,000 students: www.adelaide.edu.au

CHILDCARE

As you would expect in a cosmopolitan city, there is a wide range of childcare facilities within the city and suburbs. Check local papers and *Yellow Pages*, or refer to: www.careforkids.co.au

30
Living in Canberra and Australian Capital Territory

State: Australian Capital Territory
Size: 2,4000 (smallest state in Australia)
Capital: Canberra
Population: 310,000
Time zone: + 9 GMT
Telephone area code: + 61 2

AUSTRALIAN CAPITAL TERRITORY

Australian Capital Territory (ACT) is the smallest of Australia's States and Territories. It is tiny by Australian standards and lies within the New South Wales borders. Its capital Canberra and surrounding suburbs are in the north east of the territory, while the Namadgi National Park occupies the whole south western area.

CANBERRA

Canberra is one of only a few purpose built capital cities in the world and the only major inland city in Australia. It used to be little more than a sheep station and farm country until Walter Burley Griffin won the Federal Capital Design Competition. Launched by King O'Malley, Minister for Home Affairs, in May 1911, the competition challenged locals to design the new city. The winner, Griffin, then went on to oversee the development

243

of the city from his plans to the impressive city that it is today. Canberra's layout and urban landscape reflect its major role as the seat of Federal Parliament and home to the national institutions that support it.

It's been called 'Australia's most liveable city' because of its natural beauty, peaceful parks, sparkling lakes, sporting facilities, all close to a modern city centre. Average commuting time from or to work is less than 20 minutes and it is less than a three-hour drive to Sydney. It is a modern, vibrant city that is extremely safe and pleasant to live in.

Canberra's population is over 300,000 and it is home to many national buildings including the National Library, the National Gallery, the High Court of Australia and Parliament House. The city enjoys a thriving arts, music and café scene. It is sometimes called 'the bush capital' because pockets of bushland reserve extend almost to the city centre and over half the land is classified as national park or nature reserve.

THE HISTORY

The Commonwealth of Australia was established by an Act of British Parliament on 1 January 1901. The first meeting of the Federal Cabinet discussed the need to create a central seat of power from which the federal States of Australia are governed. This spawned the contentious issue of which city would become the nation's capital. Arch rivals Sydney and Melbourne were both desperate to win this honour and, as no agreement could be reached, Canberra was declared the new capital due to being strategically located between the two competitors.

THE CLIMATE

There are four distinct seasons in Canberra. Spring and autumn are extremely pleasant. Winter in Canberra can be cold but the sky is usually blue and sunny. Summer temperatures can be quite high.

THE ATTRACTIONS

Parliament House

This building is the focal point for Canberra. Built in 1988, into the peak of Capital Hill, it is a modern structure set in the middle of 23 hectares of native gardens, topped with a grass-covered roof on which you're allowed to walk. Visitors are allowed to observe Question Time when Parliament is sitting; alternatively you can view some of the wonderful modern art that is on display.

Embassy spotting

Visitors can easily spend an afternoon touring Canberra's 70 foreign embassies. Yarralumla, Red Hill and Forrest are where most are located, and many of the buildings are visually impressive and worth taking the time to view.

National Gallery of Australia

The National Gallery is home to the finest modern art collection in the southern hemisphere. It has more than 70,000 works which range from European old masters to contemporary Aboriginal artists. The gallery is also home to internationally renowned collections including Jackson Pollock's *Blue Poles*. Home to one of the most impressive permanent collections in the country, the NGA is an essential stop for lovers of Australian art. Other masterpieces include Lucian Freud's *After Cezanne*, and works by de Kooning and Reubens. The Sculpture Garden is worth taking a stroll through, showcasing pieces by local sculptors.

High Court

Next door to the gallery is the High Court of Australia. This impressive venue has three courtrooms which have been the venue of many of the country's most historical judgements over the past 30 years. Members of the public are permitted to sit in on hearings when the court is in session.

National Botanic Gardens

Situated on the slopes of Black Mountain, and spreading over 50 hectares, the Gardens contain over 6,000 species of native flora. The eucalypt forest alone has over 600 species. Take a walk through the misted rainforest and a tour of the medicinal plants used in years past by the Aborigines.

The Australian War Memorial

This commemorates all Australians who lost their lives in war. The intricately built Hall of Memory is the focus of the memorial and its beautiful interior features a dome made of six million Italian mosaic pieces.

Events

Canberra Day is held on the third Monday in March each year, and in celebration the city holds a ten-day festival to mark the occasion. The Canberra Festival celebrates the city's birthday with a combination of music, food, a Mardi Gras, displays and a parade. March also brings the huge National Folk Festival to Canberra.

Surrounding areas

Canberra's relationship with its natural environment sets it apart from other world capitals. Canberra's open space network is world-renowned, with over half of the ACT classed as national park or nature reserve. Canberra is central to interstate attractions with the golden beaches of the South Coast and the ski-fields of the magnificent Snowy Mountains, both no more than two hours' car travel away.

Wineries

Even Canberra's numerous politicians can't polish off the two million bottles of wine which are produced annually in the Australian Capital Territory (ACT) each year. Wine is a huge export industry for the Territory. The ACT wine regions of Hall, Lake George and Murrumbateman can all be accessed in a 90-minutes' drive from Canberra, and the wineries offer cellar-door tastings.

FOOD AND DRINK

Due to the large proportion of politicians and high profile businessmen frequenting the area, dining out in central Canberra is a more formal experience than in other Australian cities. There are many leading restaurants, which tend to be on the expensive side. Civic is the centre for fine dining with Kingston and Manuka offering some alternatives. All cuisine styles are catered for, and more affordable eateries can be found throughout the city and suburbs.

SHOPPING

There are two main shopping centres in Canberra. The Woden Plaza has recently undergone vast refurbishment, offering the widest and most comprehensive shopping and leisure experiences in the ACT. All big name Australian brands can be found there, alongside many small local boutiques. The Canberra Centre, in the heart of the CBD, is a large mall which houses David Jones and Myer alongside many other high street shops.

THE SUBURBS

The artificial Lake Burley Griffin is the focal point of the city with everything built around it. The northern side of the lake is the Civic area which has many shops and businesses, the university and suburbs such as Turner, Acton and Reid. South of the lake are the Parliamentary and administrative buildings which are surrounded by suburbs including Barton, Deakin and Parkes. Interestingly the current Prime Minister, John Howard, prefers to live in a stunning mansion overlooking Sydney harbour rather than in the official residence in the Canberra suburb of Yarralumla!

GETTING AROUND

Despite being a planned city, it is easy to get lost in Canberra. Therefore it's a good idea to get your bearings on arrival by hopping on to the Canberra Explorer bus. The driver's commentary throughout the one-hour trip will provide a useful overview of the city.

Due to the low population, getting around is easy and traffic jams are virtually unheard of in Canberra where the average commute time is less than 20 minutes. Sydney is only three hours by car with Melbourne reachable within an eight hour drive.

Bus

Canberra has no local rail or tram network, so most people get around using the ACTION buses (Australian Capital Territory Internal Omnibus

Network) which run fairly frequently. Long-distance buses depart from the Jolimont Centre on Northbourne Avenue to destinations across Australia.

Train

Countylink offers a train service between Canberra and Sydney. The station is located on Wentworth Avenue in Kingston. Trains depart several times a day and the journey takes around four hours. There are also routes to Melbourne; however, they are not direct and will require at least one change.

Taxis

Taxis can be flagged down easily on the street or can be pre-booked:

- Canberra Cabs 13 2227

Bicycle

Canberra is a haven for cyclists. There are many well-built bike paths and plenty of attractive landscapes and greenery to gaze at.

Car rental

www.vroomvroomvroom.com.au will enable you to search for the best car rental deals in Canberra.

RENTING A HOME IN CANBERRA

There is a buoyant rental market in Canberra and you shouldn't have any problems in finding a good quality home at an affordable price, with rents cheaper than in Sydney and Melbourne.

The *Canberra Times* newspaper has the definitive residential real estate guide (Saturday editions) in which you'll find a comprehensive listing of all residential properties for sale, rent or lease. The *Canberra Real Estate Guide* is another publication available from most Canberra real estate agents.

Also refer to:

- www.canberraexchange.com.au

- www.propertyguide.com.au

USEFUL INFORMATION

Canberra Airport is well serviced by leading airlines with routes to most Australian capitals. For international or regional destinations, you'll have to catch a connecting flight from Sydney. The airport is about eight minutes' drive from the centre of Canberra, and cheap to get to by taxi.

31
Working and Studying in Canberra

COST OF LIVING

Canberra's cost of living compares favourably with other Australian cities, being cheaper than most. Housing, entertainment and recreation are all more affordable than many of the other State capitals.

CURRENT ECONOMIC OVERVIEW

The ACT has enjoyed vigorous economic growth in recent years and is the fastest growing of all Australian States and Territories. Canberra benefits from its strategic location within the Asia Pacific region and it has a first class infrastructure with a skilled and flexible workforce. It is increasingly being identified within Australia and internationally as an ideal location to do business. Canberra also has the highest proportion of people in all States and Territories with post-school qualifications. It has a well-earned reputation as a centre of advanced technology and claims the largest market in Australia for computers and software.

Industry profile

Canberra is the federal administrative centre for the nation and government administration employs many of the region's workers. Other leading occupations in the region include nursing, computing professionals, general clerks and teachers. The largest industries consist of government administration, defence and school education.

EMPLOYMENT OPPORTUNITIES

Canberra is a much smaller city than any of the other Australian State capitals and has a highly skilled and specialised workforce in place. Therefore there are fewer employment opportunities for migrants – especially if their experience is gained in occupations outside the above industries. If you are considering moving to Canberra for work, please ensure that you research whether your occupation is in demand as your skills may be better suited to another part of Australia where work is more readily available. Canberra is the only city in Australia that was purpose built for government administration.

Your job search

- The *Canberra Times* is the local newspaper, which provides a valuable insight into the area and more specifically, current local employment opportunities.

- Canberra Connect is the government site that has links to employment sites and Canberra based jobs: www.canberraconnect.act.gov.au

- Jobsguide can help you with your job search in the ACT and across all of Australia: www.jobsguide.com.au

EDUCATION

Primary

All children in the ACT who are already 5, or turning 5 before 30 April, are required to enrol at primary school. Children attend until they are old enough to go to high school.

Secondary

Secondary school is called high school in the ACT. High schools are for children aged from about 12 to 16 years. High school goes from Year 7 to Year 10 and the subjects taught vary from school to school so do check what they are teaching in your chosen location.

Universities

There are many study opportunities in Canberra, including the Australian National University, Canberra University and Canberra Institute of TAFE.

www.decs.act.gov.au is the website for the Department of Education and Training for the Australian Capital Territory – it includes a list of schools within the area.

32
Tasmania

State: Tasmania 'The Apple Isle'
Size: 67,800 sq kms
Capital: Hobart
Population: 200,000
Time zone: 10 + GMT
Telephone area code: +61 3

It is as pleasing a town as any that I know. It is beautifully situated.

Anthony Trollope on Hobart, 1871.

Most people are familiar with the major Australian cities but the mention of Tasmania leads to confusion as to where and what it is!

With a population of just under half a million, Tasmania is the island state of Australia and consists of more than 300 islands and is just about as far down under as you can go in Australia. It is a beautiful land of spectacular coastlines, rugged mountains, stunning wilderness and beautiful lakes.

www.discovertasmania.com.au

TASMANIA

There are four major population centres – Hobart, Launceston, Burnie and Devonport.

Hobart

Hobart is the state capital of Tasmania, and is the smallest and most southerly of all Australia's capitals. Home to around 200,000 people, Hobart is located on the south east coast of the island and has pretty beaches scattered along the coastline. It is an aesthetically appealing city, set on a beautiful harbour, overlooked by soaring mountains and filled with a higher proportion of its original buildings than any other major city. Hobart has striking similarities to charming old British coastal towns and the most well preserved colonial heritage listed buildings in all of Australia. Historically, it is the second oldest city in Australia and has close links with the sea. The prestigious annual Sydney–Hobart boat race is undoubtedly the most high profile sporting event on the Tasmanian calendar and attracts crowds from around the world who turn out in their thousands every Christmas to see the incredible boats swarm into the harbour.

Aside from the boat race, Tasmania has a strong sporting tradition with state of the art facilities to match. It also has a vibrant cultural scene with a thriving theatre community including Australia's oldest theatre, The Theatre Royal, which is Tasmania's hub for live music, music and dance. Hobart is also home to one of the best small orchestras in the world, not to mention art house cinemas, museums and art galleries.

The waterfront has the hustle and bustle that comes from being a busy port, and it is the focus for Hobart's attractions and a lively and fun area to eat, drink and shop in. The cool, clean environment yields internationally sought after gourmet foods and wines, both of which are plentiful in this underrated State. Retail and tourism are also major employers in the Hobart region, with the largest secondary industries being food and beverage manufacturing and electricity supply.

Launceston

Launceston, the State's second largest city, with its graceful Victorian architecture and green parks, sits inland of the Tamar River. It is the gateway to Tasmania's premier wine growing region – the Tamar Valley. Launceston's industrial base is concentrated in food, beverages and metals manufacturing.

Burnie

Burnie is a regional city that has a large port with cargo shipping being the major industry in the area. There's plenty to do for locals and visitors, with easy access to both sand and surf close by. The scenery around the region is nothing short of spectacular, and the beautiful waterfalls are worth a visit. Nature lovers should head east of the city to Fernglade, a tranquil retreat along the banks of the Emu River where you might be lucky enough to see a wild platypus.

Others places of interest include Burnie Park, the Emu Valley Rhododendron Garden, the Lactos Cheese Factory and the Pioneer Village Museum.

Devonport

Devonport is a small town with a population of around 25,000. It is a gateway to Tasmania and can be reached by travelling by ferry across the Bass Strait from Melbourne in Victoria. From the continental mainland, you can cross the strait with your car from Melbourne on the overnight vehicle ferry, the *Spirit of Tasmania*. It is an active seaport and has some interesting cultural attractions including the Tasmanian Aboriginal Culture and Art Centre which holds a decent collection of Aboriginal rock engravings and the Tasmanian Maritime and Port Museum.

THE CLIMATE

Tasmania has a temperate maritime climate with four distinct seasons. Hobart is said to receive more sunshine each day and less than half the annual rainfall than Sydney. It is not uncommon for snow to fall on Tasmania's highlands, but rarely in major towns.

THE ATTRACTIONS

Nearly 40% of the State is protected wilderness, marine reserve, nature reserve or forest. In fact, much of the area is considered of such environmental significance that it has been granted World Heritage status.

Battery Point

Battery Point is Hobart's most historic suburb, and retains the character of a Cornish fishing village of the last century.

Port Arthur

Port Arthur is Tasmania's top tourist attraction and an area of considerable historical significance. In 1830 it was established as a convict settlement and became the largest in Australia until it was closed in 1877. Dubbed 'hell on earth' by the inmates, much of Port Arthur's original buildings remain and are open to the public.

GETTING AROUND

Tasmania has well-developed air and sea links to the rest of Australia and the world. Nearly 500 flights each week carry passengers and airfreight to and from four airports, the largest being Hobart, which is approximately one hour by air from Melbourne and one hour 40 minutes from Sydney. Car and bus travel are the most common forms of transport in Tasmania as there are no train routes in operation.

For detailed bus information refer to: www.metrotas.com.au

You can travel to Tasmania via boat from both Melbourne and Sydney. The *Spirit of Tasmania* operate both routes. For fares and further information refer to: www.spiritoftasmania.com.au

COST OF LIVING

The cost of living in Tasmania is considerably lower than other Australian cities and housing is particularly affordable. Property in Hobart is generally less than half the price of an equivalent home in Sydney, ensuring a good standard of living for residents. As with most other Australian cities, Tasmania offers diverse lifestyle options ensuring there is something to suit everyone's tastes and needs including inner-city, suburban, beachside and rural suburbs. Tasmania also has the enviable position of having the lowest crime rate in Australia and its unique position ensures that it is one of the safest places in the world to live.

• Property website: www.realestate.com.au and click on to TAS.

IF YOU ARE CONSIDERING MIGRATING

Useful information can be obtained from:
www.dpac.tas.gov.au/divisions/multitas/migrating.html

WORKING IN TASMANIA

Employment opportunities

Tasmania's economy has developed rapidly in recent years, which has led to skills shortages across a number of professions and trades, creating new opportunities for skilled migrants. Check the immigration website to check both the Skilled Occupation List and the current Occupations in Demand in Tasmania.

Brit tip

If there is little chance of you gaining a visa for one of Australia's more popular cities such as Melbourne, Perth and Sydney, then it may be worth your while considering Tasmania. You may be able to score extra points for settling outside of metropolitan areas and there is the scope to move elsewhere after an agreed amount of time spent working in the area.

If you are a prospective skilled migrant who wishes to settle anywhere in Tasmania, the Department of Economic Development can nominate/sponsor your visa application through the STNI or SIR visa schemes.

Applicants with skills in demand within Tasmania will be given preference, although people with other occupations will be considered if they can demonstrate that they are able to settle and secure skilled employment, or start a business, easily.

For further information: www.development.tas.gov.au

For those on Working Holiday Visas, it is worth knowing that there are employment opportunities all year round in the Tasmanian harvest labour industry. For more information contact the National Harvest Labour Information Service (NHLIS). You can call free from anywhere in Australia (1800 062 332).

For information on employment opportunities in Tasmania refer to the government website which contains a wealth of useful information and links: www.service.tas.gov.au.

Other useful sites

- www.bluecollar.com.au This site contains useful information about wages in Tasmania and also has a list of current vacancies in the cities and surrounds.

- For further information on working in Tasmania: www.development.tas.gov.au and click on 'migrating to Tasmania'.

EDUCATION

In Tasmania it is compulsory that all children between the ages of 5 and 16 must be enrolled at a school or receive home education.

For further information about schooling refer to: www.education.tas.gov.au

University

Tasmania is home to one of the oldest universities in Australia – The University of Tasmania: www.utas.edu.au

USEFUL INFORMATION

- Standard Time in Tasmania is ten hours ahead of Greenwich Mean Time (GMT+10). They do observe Daylight Saving so the time is shifted forward by one hour, resulting in a 11-hour difference ahead of Greenwich Mean time (GMT+11). Tasmania's daylight saving begins on the first Sunday in October and ends on the last Sunday in March.

- The International dialling code for Tasmania is +61 3.

33
Making the Move

So you've done the research, discovered you are eligible for a visa and reached the monumental decision to move to Australia. What now?

SEEKING PROFESSIONAL HELP

As this book has shown, Australia's migration rules are complex and can be subject to frequent change. Therefore, potential migrants may choose to seek the assistance of a migration agent who can help assess the chances of success. In theory, they also should be able to ensure that the whole process is more efficient and faster than going it alone.

A migration agent can advise you precisely which visa is right for you and your circumstances. This is crucial as an application can only be considered under the visa type you selected and, if this turns out not to be the correct one for you, it will be declined and you will need to apply again – wasting both time and money. However, it is worth noting that if you have carried out your research thoroughly ahead of your visa application, there is no reason for you to get this wrong.

A word of warning

Whilst using an agent can help the process, migration agents *cannot* influence the outcome of your application. The decision on your application will depend solely on whether all of the relevant documentation

261

and information has been provided within the set time limits, and on your application meeting the criteria for the specific visa applied for.

How to choose an agent

There are many agents advertising their services on the web and in print so choosing one can be confusing. If you decide to go down this route then look out for the following.

Registration

If you are using an Australian based agent, they must be registered with the Migration Agents Registration Authority. This is a protection for consumers as those agents who are found to be dishonest or incompetent can be punished and prevented from further practice.

Shop around

Take time to compare agents and what services they are offering so that you find one that is right for your personal needs. Remember all cases are different so confirm that they have experience in your field. Do ensure that they provide you with information about all the fees ahead of making any commitment, and get this in writing. Also, do not be afraid to ask about their success rate. If they are a reputable company they should not be afraid of telling you how good they are.

Some points of reference

Please note that these are not personal recommendations, merely examples of the migration services available:

- www.australiamigrate.co.uk
- www.australianmigrationspecialists.com.au
- www.visabureau.co.uk/australia

TIME LINE

If you have a clear idea of when you would like to leave the country, ensure that you have a realistic time line in place. Check with immigration as to how long your visa application is likely to take and whether or not it should be straightforward. If you are moving your family, my advice is to plan as far ahead as possible and allow more time than you think you need for unforeseen issues.

Brit tip

If you book travel to Australia months in advance, try to book a flexible ticket so that you are not committed to departing on a particular date, as it will be hard to predict the day your visa is granted.

BUDGET

The visa application can be expensive – especially if you run into complications. Make sure you are aware of all the costs that are involved. Don't forget the additional expenses of relocating including removals, shipping, and customs. If you intend to rent a home immediately upon arrival you will need at least a month's rent money at your disposal to cover the bond.

IF YOU HAVE CHILDREN

Moving is a stressful experience for all concerned and emotions can run high – especially if you are moving your entire family. Therefore, make sure your children are prepared as far ahead as possible for the move. For some useful tips, refer to:

www.overseas-emigration.co.uk/prepchild.php

CUSTOMS

Australia has very strict customs which must be adhered to. Failure to do so may lead to your belongings being impounded. It is your responsibility to ensure that you are aware of current customs regulations and how they may affect you. For further information, refer to the traveller section of the Australian customs website: www.customs.gov.au

REMOVAL COMPANIES

Unless you are starting your trip to Australia as backpackers, you are likely to have excess baggage or belongings that you will need to send separately. Most people do this ahead of departure so it is at least en route when you arrive. You can send your belongings via ship or air. Shipping is often the cheaper option as it takes longer and you purchase crate space which can be shared with others. Sending items by air is of course a faster option but can be expensive as freight companies usually charge by weight. You need to work out what you want to send and how you want to send it before contacting removal companies. It is advisable to contact two or three reputable companies to get a quote. Be sure to ask how long it will take, including customs, processing on arrival in Australia and whether your items will be insured.

For an idea of the removal services available refer to:

• www.removals-shipping.co.uk

• www.britannia-movers.co.uk

Relocation companies

Start right is an executive relocation company which, for a fee, will assist your move to Australia above and beyond removals. They offer a variety of services which include helping you find a home, school etc. If you are interested refer to their website: www.startright.com.au

---

Brit tip

- Make a comprehensive list of what you have packed in each box and number them accordingly. This will help in the event of any customs issues.

- If you use a removal company, you can save yourself money by purchasing your own boxes and packing items yourself – however, do make sure you follow their guidelines.

- Take the least amount you can with you as goods are not expensive in Australia and your old belongings may not suit your new lifestyle.

- If avoidable, do not take British electrics as Australian plugs are different from ours and you will need lots of adaptors or pay for plugs to be changed.

PAPERWORK

Aside from your travel documents, I strongly advise that you ensure you have the originals or at least copies of all of your other important pieces of paperwork including:

- birth certificates

- marriage certificate

- driving licence

- qualifications (educational and professional)

You will need as much identification as possible when opening a bank account etc and potential employers (particularly in professional services such as banking) may ask you to provide such items as documentary evidence. Do also take medical certificates or documents if you have an existing medical condition.

If you have children of school age, ensure that you have evidence of your child's academic records and qualifications.

Brit tip

If you are considering owning a car in Australia, do take evidence of your no claims bonus should you have one. Insurers do reduce premiums by up to 50% for good drivers.

FURTHER INFORMATION

The Emigrate/Opportunities Abroad Show

This show is the world's biggest emigration event which aims to provide people with the opportunity to find out all you need to know about a new life overseas. Migration experts are on hand as are ex-pats who can share their own personal experiences with you. They also have seminars that discuss moving to particular countries, which includes Australia.

To find out when the next show is, refer to: www.outboundpublishing.com

Fresh Start Show

This is an annual event which aims to inform anyone thinking of living and working abroad on how to begin their process. Experts are on hand to offer advice on the visas, education, tax, removals etc. To find out details of their 2006 event refer to: www.freshstartshow.co.uk

All that remains to be said is good luck, be sure to pack your sun block and see you down under!

34
Slang

For some of us Brits, our only experience of Australians and their language is from watching *Home and Away* and *Neighbours*, neither of which present a fair representation of the Aussie language. (However, I can confirm that the wonderful Aussie mullet is well and truly alive and being sported by more men than it should be.)

In fact, more than half of the population of Australia speak languages other than English, including Italian, Lebanese and Greek, so anyone who is expecting to hear 'crikey' and 'possum' in every sentence is in for a surprise!

The true Aussie language is full of colloquial expressions, slang words and slang phrases which locals have adopted into their daily language.

TOP THREE EXPRESSIONS

Here are a few words and phrases that might be useful to you.

No worries	Expression of reassurance (not a problem; forget about it; I can do it; yes, I'll do it)
Good on yer	Well done – good for you
Fair dinkum	Fair enough – ok

A TO Z OF COMMON AUSSIE SLANG

Aggro	angry/aggressive
Amber nectar	beer
Arvo	afternoon
Aussie (pronounced Ozzie)	Australian
Barbie	the famous Aussie word for barbecue
Battler	working class Aussie trying to make ends meet
Beaut or You beauty	great, fantastic
Billabong	watering hole
Billy	teapot, container for boiling water (useful in the outback)
Bloody oath!	that's the truth
Bludger	a lazy person or someone who doesn't work
Bogan	person who takes little pride in his appearance, spends his days slacking and drinking beer
Bonzer	excellent – very good
Boogie board	half-sized surf board
Boomer	a large male kangaroo
Bottle shop	known to us as off licences – the only places you can buy wine/beer/spirits as you can't buy them in supermarkets
Bottle O	abbreviation of bottle shop
Brizzie	Brisbane, state capital of Queensland
Brumby	a wild horse
Bundy	short for Bundaberg, Queensland – the name of a rum that is a favourite Aussie tipple (mixed with coke)
Bush	anywhere that isn't in town (in particular refers to the outback)
Chips	Confusingly fall into two categories – hot chips are as you'd expect in Britain, the deep fried potato version, and cold chips are crisps to you and me

Chuck a sickie	take the day off sick from work when you're perfectly healthy – it's an Aussie tradition, and considered an essential and acceptable part of working life
Coathanger	a term of endearment for Sydney Harbour bridge
Cobber	a friend or mate
Cockie	cockatoo – these are native birds in Australia – or cockroach: get used to them, they are a way of life in most parts of Australia and on the large side
Coldie	a beer
Cozzie	swimming costume
Crook	ill/sick
Dag	a nerd
Digger	an old soldier
Dill	idiot
Dob (somebody) in	inform on somebody – tell a tale
Drongo	idiot
Dunny	toilet
Esky	large insulated food/drink container for picnics, barbecues etc (what we call ice boxes)
Fair dinkum	true, genuine
Fair go	give us a break
Feral	wild
Flake	shark meat
Floater	a meat pie with mushy peas (a traditional Aussie delicacy)
G'day	hello!
Gabba	Wooloongabba – the Brisbane cricket ground (a holy place to some Aussies apparently)
Galah	idiot – named after the noisy birds of the same name
Go off	usually used in the context 'that party went off' – ie it was wild
Grog	liquor, beer

Have a dig	make an attempt
Joey	a baby kangaroo
Kick in	put in money/contribute
Knockabout	funny guy
Larrikin	a bloke who is known for being a joker/prankster
Lay by	putting something on hold at a shop for you to collect at a later date
Lollies	we call them sweets/candy – the Aussies call them lollies (bizarrely even if they are not actually lollipops)
Little Johnny	an affectionate term for the Prime Minister John Howard
Middy	285ml beer glass
Milkbar	corner shop
Muddy	mud crab (a great Aussie delicacy)
Nipper	young surf lifesaver
No drama(s)	whatever you are referring to is not an issue
Ocker	down to earth Aussie man
Outback	remote parts of Australia
Oz	Australia!
Pash	refers to a kiss or kissing
Pokies	poker machines, fruit machines, gambling slot machines
Polly	politician
Pom, pommy	an Englishman
Rack off	go away
Rego	vehicle registration
Ripper	great, fantastic
Roo	kangaroo
Salvos	member of the Salvation Army
Sanger	a sausage
Schoolie's week	a highlight of the school year for pupils where the school leavers all go away for a week together to celebrate the end of school!

Schooner	large beer glass
Scratchy	an instant lottery ticket
Servo	petrol station
Sheila	a woman
Sickie	day off sick from work when you aren't ill
Smoko	smoke or coffee break
Snag	another word for sausage – you will also hear the term Sausage Sizzler which is a sausage sandwich hot off the grill
(A) spunk	a handsome male
Strewth	my goodness
Strides	trousers
Stubby	a 375ml beer bottle
Stubby holder	polystyrene insulated holder to keep beer cold – a must have item for real Aussie males
Sunbake	sunbathing
Taswegian	derogatory term for a person from Tasmania
Thongs	not underwear! The British equivalent is 'flip flops'
Tinny	can of beer or a small aluminium boat
True blue	patriotic
Tucker	food
Two up	traditional gambling game played by spinning two coins simultaneously
Unit	flat, apartment
Ute	utility vehicle, pickup truck
Vinnie's	St Vincent De Paul's (charity thrift stores and hostels)
Walkabout	a lengthy walk somewhere
Wog	person of Mediterranean origin, affectionately used and considered far less insulting than the same word in the UK
Yabby	a small freshwater crayfish – common seafood dish
Yakka	work

Take more of your money with you

If you're planning a move to Australia it's likely that the last thing on your mind is foreign exchange. However, at some point you will have to change your hard earned money into dollars. Unfortunately, exchange rates are constantly moving and as a result can have a big impact on the amount of money you have to create your dream home.

For example, if you look at the Australian dollar during 2005 you can see how this movement can affect you. Sterling against the dollar was as high as 2.4879 and as low as 2.2761. So if you had £200,000 to transfer you could have received as much as $497,580 or as little as $455,220 – a difference of over $42,000.

It is possible to avoid this pitfall by fixing a rate through a **forward contract**. A small deposit will secure you a rate for anywhere up to 2 years in advance and by doing so provides the security of having the currency you need at a guaranteed cost.

Another option if you have time on your side is a **limit order**. This is used when you want to achieve a rate that is currently not available. You set the rate that you want and the market is then monitored. As soon as that rate is achieved the currency is purchased for you.

If you need to act swiftly and your capital is readily available then it is most likely that you will use a **spot transaction**. This is the *Buy now, Pay now* option where you get the most competitive rate on the day.

To ensure you get the most for your money it's a good idea to use a foreign exchange specialist such as Currencies Direct. As an alternative to your bank, Currencies Direct is able to offer you extremely competitive exchange rates, no commission charges and free transfers*. This can mean considerable savings on your transfer when compared to using a bank.

*Over £5,000

Information provided by Currencies Direct.
Website: *www.currenciesdirect.com*
Email: *info@currenciesdirect.com*
Tel: 0845 389 1729

Index